Sailing in the fog

Sailing in the fog

THE SEAMANSHIP SERIES

Roger F. Duncan

INTERNATIONAL MARINE
PUBLISHING COMPANY
Camden, Maine 04843

To Mary Chandler Duncan

©1986 by International Marine Publishing Company
Second printing 1986.

Typeset by The Key Word, Inc., Belchertown, Massachusetts
Printed and bound by BookCrafters, Inc., Chelsea, Michigan

Published by International Marine Publishing Company
21 Elm Street, Camden, Maine 04843
(207) 236-4342

Library of Congress Cataloging in Publication Data

Duncan, Roger F.
  Sailing in the fog.

  Includes index.
  (The Seamanship series)
  1. Navigation. 2. Fog. I. Title.
VK559.D77 1986   623.89   85-23957
ISBN 0-87742-208-7

Contents

Preface

This book is written for the skipper or navigator who plans a cruise in waters where fog is prevalent and who has had little experience with it. The first part of the book deals with the instruments he may use and with their limitations. The second part of the book recognizes that there is no substitute for experience and seeks to introduce the reader vicariously to the kinds of occurrences he may expect, through accounts of actual runs in the fog, two of them built around literal logbook entries.

Much of this book is not easy armchair adventure. Parts of it must be studied and the reasoning followed through. Logbook accounts must be read with careful reference to the charts and with considerable imagination. It is my hope that anyone who reads the book as carefully as it was written, while he may not welcome a foggy day, will accept it with the confidence that its end will find him anchored in a safe harbor.

Most of the book seems to be concerned with Maine fogs because most of my experience has been on that coast. Of course fog prevails in many other parts of the world where warm, damp air blows over cold water. I have seen it in Chesapeake Bay in the fall. The coasts of Nova Scotia, Newfoundland, and Iceland are well-known examples. The Bering Sea, Aleutian Islands, and the West Coast of North America south almost to Mexico are in the same situation. Here the Japan Current warms the offshore waters, and westerly winds carry warm air inshore over colder water flowing south from the Arctic. The southern hemisphere has parallel cases off the southwest coast of Africa and the southern coast of Chile. Dense fogs form in the English Channel and the North Sea in winter and early spring when southwest winds blow over colder water pouring out of the Baltic Sea. In summer, fog is much less frequent over England and Scotland because the Gulf Stream warms these waters more or less uniformly. Fog then is more like haze, drizzle, light rain, and low cloud. Indeed, the British definition of fog is visibility below 1,000 meters, half a mile. Whatever the cause of fog, when it shuts down in any longitude, it looks the same, is equally unnerving, and can be dealt with in the same way.

Any reader with questions, comments, additions, or experiences relevant to the subject of this book is urged to write to me. I will welcome such correspondence enthusiastically.

Roger F. Duncan
Box 66
East Boothbay, Maine 04544

1

Fog
and
the
Skipper

Fog can be terrifying. The summer sailor, out to escape the heat ashore on a muggy, hazy day, may see a bank of fog advance over the outer islands, shutting them out one by one. It pours down over the nearer land, irresistibly filling up bays and river mouths, enveloping him and his boat in a gray, dank murk, blinding him, muffling sounds, shutting him into a cold, wet world limited to the space between two wave crests. Panic may be not far off. However, there is a sure defense against fog panic, and that is the subject of this book.

First, the skipper must understand and firmly believe that fog is *not* a curse dropped on him by malevolent gods of sea and air bent on his confusion and destruction, but it is a natural phenomenon governed by physical laws utterly indifferent to him. Understanding these laws both reassures us and enables us to avoid the dangers involved. This is a "left brain" exercise. It requires the disciplined subjugation of emotion and intuition and the exercise of reason applied to factual knowledge.

How Fog Forms

In the summer, fog on the New England coast usually occurs when a large high-pressure area develops north of Bermuda. This air mass, known as the Bermuda High, is warm and soon becomes saturated with invisible water vapor as it lies over the warm ocean. Should lower pressure prevail over the New England coast, part of this air flows northward toward New England, producing hot, muggy days and sweaty nights in the cities. As this warm, damp air approaches the eastward-trending coast, it passes over cold coastal water. This water is cold partly because a branch of the Labrador Current works its way southward between the coast and the Gulf Stream and partly because the inshore water is stirred up by tidal currents so that the colder water is pushed to the surface. As the warm, saturated air passes over the cold water, the invisible vapor at lower levels condenses into tiny droplets of liquid water. A little of this is haze; a lot of it is fog.

Many of the characteristics of summer fog are predictable from this explanation. For instance, far offshore, away from the influence of coastal tidal currents, the fog is often thinner than it is in the mouths of rivers and off points where the tide runs hard. Point Lepreau in New Brunswick has been identified as the site of a major fog factory by some cruising men who have been by it many times but have never seen it. Petit Manan, Schoodic Point, the waters around Vinalhaven and Matinicus, and Cape Elizabeth support branch factories. Nantucket Sound is often foggy as the result of tidal stirring, but the water is warmer there and the fog less persistent. In general, the farther east one sails, the colder is the coastal water and the thicker and more persistent the fog.

The same situation occurs on the West Coast when a westerly wind blows over the warm offshore waters and meets colder waters inshore. San Francisco Bay and Puget Sound are notorious examples, but the phenomenon occurs all the way up the Alaskan coast.

When the air is saturated with water vapor, either a very slight drop in temperature or a slight increase in humidity will produce condensation. A slight increase in temperature or decrease in humidity on a foggy day will cause a scale-up. Often the temperature and humidity lie very close to this critical point at which fog will condense. Hence at night, when temperatures drop, the fog is likely to shut down. If the afternoon air feels damp, if the wind is coming off the water, if one can see his breath condense against the darkness of a hatch or a dark shoreline, the air is reaching the condensation point and fog is almost certain by night.

Conversely, if the sun is shining over the top of the fog in the morning, even if it is choking thick, it is quite likely to "burn off." That is, the temperature will rise to the point at which the tiny droplets will evaporate into invisible vapor. This is likely to happen first over the land, since the earth heats up more quickly than the water.

If there is any wind on such a day, the fog blowing in from the sea over a warmer island will dry up, leaving a window in the fog to leeward of the island even though it is thick all around. This may happen over even a small island, but the navigator can bet heavily on such a window to leeward of large islands such as Grand Manan, Wass Island, Isle au Haut, and through the thorofares and reaches on the Maine coast. Ipswich Bay, the north side of Cape Cod, and the waters close northward of Marthas Vineyard, Nantucket, and Block Island show the same characteristics. On a cloudy day, of course, the land warms up more slowly, and the scale-up will come later or not at all.

Often the fog will approach in a clearly defined bank, visible first as a white line in the southern sky. Overhead, rags and clumps of fog will scud across the hazy sky, and amazingly quickly as the humidity rises and the temperature falls, the fog shuts down. This often occurs when the land heats up and draws the cooler air in off the water, pulling the warmer, damp air behind it over the cool coastal water.

At other times, especially if there is little or no wind, the fog will clamp down from above. As the air cools in the afternoon, condensation begins aloft. The sun gets hazy. The air feels damp. Sneakers which have been wet with salt water become cold, wet, and clammy, and breath becomes visible. Perhaps a line of fog will appear across the top of a high island, although visibility at sea level may still be a mile. Then it is suddenly thick as tar.

On a sunny day with the sun warming the top of the fog bank and the water cooling the bottom, the fog may be only a hundred feet deep or even less. Sometimes a man at the masthead can see over the top of it. When one is approaching a high island, often the trees at the top of it will appear against the sky considerably before the shoreline shows up. The Camden Hills and the mountains of Mount Desert are often visible on a sunny day above a low, thick bank of fog.

Fog, then, is a matter of balance between temperature and humidity. Sacrifices to Poseidon will have no effect on it, but a warm sun will usually burn it off as temperatures rise, or a northwest wind will dry it up as humidity falls.

How to Plan for Fog

Long-term averages are of little value in predicting fog. The Coast Guard keeps records of the hours of operation of fog signals, and there are some interesting figures on visibilities in the appendix to the *Coast Pilot*, but they are of little help to the mariner who wants to know when to plan a cruise. The Bermuda High in a particular year may form early in June or not until August. The northward flow of warm air may be frequently interrupted by cold fronts bringing cool, dry air out of Canada to the northwest or by occasional dry easterlies. In general, based on a prejudice developed over a number of years, I prefer to cruise in New England in June, early July, late August, and September. The weather patterns seem to move more quickly at these times, the winds are brisker, and the weather changes are more pronounced from day to day. In late July and early August the weather tends to stagnate, and there is little wind and more fog. At any time during the cruising season, however, the fog may shut down.

If Cautious Conrad decides to wait it out until he has good visibility, he may lie at anchor until he grounds on his own beer cans. His too-short vacation may be wasted on a very short cruise with intervals of cabin fever. Fog on the coasts of North America may last a few hours or, with occasional scale-ups, two weeks, depending on the stability of the Bermuda High or the North Pacific High and the advance of weather fronts across the continent. The wise mariner will learn to deal with fog by the intelligent application of immutable physical laws. After all, a great many people have navigated the New England coast safely with far less knowledge and fewer instruments than are available to the modern yachtsman. Therefore, except on a really impossible day, the skipper who faces the fog with knowledge and confidence can plan to get underway.

2

The Compass

The first and most important resource for the mariner beset by fog is a good compass properly mounted and accurately compensated.

Fundamentally, the compass has not come far from the magnetized needle inserted in a straw floating in a bowl of water that guided the late medieval mariner along the shores of Europe and far out into the Atlantic. Nowadays the needle is attached to a card balanced on a jeweled bearing. The bowl of water is now a bowl of highly refined oil that will not freeze or thicken with cold and yet will steady the movement of the card. Modern compasses are usually enclosed in a plastic sphere to give the card freedom to tip within the bowl instead of having the whole instrument in gimbals. Also, the sphere acts as a magnifier so that the far side of the card appears to be much bigger to the helmsman than it really is. But the modern compass is still a floating needle, and it still aligns itself as reliably with the earth's magnetic field as it ever did.

Compass Selection

There are several considerations in buying a compass, and the last of them is price. First consider size. Any compass will point north in the showroom, but aboard your boat, hard on the wind in the choppy waters of a tide rip, will it point consistently north steadily enough so that you can steer a course by it? The bigger the instrument is, the better will the card be damped and the more steadily will it lie. On the other hand, a six-inch compass may be more than you really need in a 20-foot boat never used far from home. For most yachts, something between a 3½-inch and a 6-inch card is acceptable.

While many able seamen have navigated every sea, bay, and gulf on the globe with flat-topped compasses, a spherical compass is probably a better instrument because there is more fluid in it to damp the action of the card and because there is less tendency for the fluid to swirl around inside a sphere than inside a flat-topped bowl. Some compasses with spherical tops are truncated (cut off flat underneath the card), making them less expensive but robbing them of some of the advantage of the truly spherical form. It may be difficult to identify a truncated compass, but the instruction sheet that comes with it should tell you.

There isn't much you can tell about a compass by looking at the outside of it, but there are a few obvious things worth checking. Rotate the compass slowly on its axis. Watch the card closely to see if it appears to waver due to irregularities in the shape or thickness of the sphere. Turn it again, watching to see if the card steadily points north while the bowl turns. If it sticks or shows a tendency to follow the bowl, turn your back on it at once.

Look at the lubber line, the line on the inside of the bowl showing the direction of the ship's head. If, when you tilt the compass, the lubber line remains perpendicular to the card, the compass is internally gimballed; that is, there is a pair of gimbal rings inside the bowl. If the lubber line tilts with the bowl, the compass is not internally gimballed. Most such compasses are built with the card floating on a jewelled bearing atop a vertical post. If the bowl is tilted slightly, the card continues to float horizontally on the post. If the bowl is sharply tilted or remains tilted for some time, the card either tilts or strikes the post and sticks. Such compasses are less expensive and are intended primarily for powerboats, which seldom heel sharply or for an extended period. Internally gimballed compasses are preferred for sailing vessels because the gimbals maintain the post in a vertical position under the horizontal card.

Some compasses, particularly the old flat-topped compasses, are externally gimballed; that is, they are supported in the binnacle by a pair of gimbal rings outside the compass bowl. These compasses have proved satisfactory for years, but are seldom seen now.

Next, hold a piece of steel near the compass and deflect the card 3 degrees, then let it return to normal. It should turn back directly, without moving beyond the proper bearing and then oscillating back again.

Now consider how the compass will fit into your cockpit. We will discuss different ways of mounting the compass later, but for the present you must decide the position of the instrument relative to the helmsman. The card must be clearly legible from the helmsman's position. This means that distance and viewing angle will be critical factors. Anywhere from 1½ to 4 feet from the helmsman is reasonable for a four-inch compass. If the helmsman will be to one side of the compass, the instrument should have lubber lines not only dead ahead but at 45 degrees to either side. If you intend to leave the compass permanently in place, you will want a flush mounting to fit into binnacle, deck, or bulkhead. If you want to take it below when it is not in use or take it ashore for safekeeping, it should be provided with a bracket mounting. More on these subjects shortly.

Provision should be made to light the compass at night. A very dim red light that lights the card but does not shine

NORTH	0	EAST	90	SOUTH	180	WEST	270
N. ¼ E.	2¾	E. ¼ S.	93	S. ¼ W.	182¾	W. ¼ N.	272¾
N. ½ E.	5½	E. ½ S.	95½	S. ½ W.	185½	W. ½ N.	275½
N. ¾ E.	8¼	E. ¾ S.	98½	S. ¾ W.	188½	W. ¾ N.	278½
N. by E.	11¼	E. by S.	101¼	S. by W.	191¼	W. by N.	281¼
N. by E. ¼ E.	14	E. by S. ¼ S.	104	S. by W. ¼ W.	194	W. by N. ¼ N.	284
N. by E. ½ E.	17	E. by S. ½ S.	107	S. by W. ½ W.	197	W. by N. ½ N.	287
N. by E. ¾ E.	20	E. by S. ¾ S.	109¾	S. by W. ¾ W.	199¾	W. by N. ¾ N.	290
N. N. E.	22½	E. S. E.	112½	S. S. W.	202½	W. N. W.	292½
N. E. by N. ¾ N.	25	S. E. by E. ¾ E.	115¼	S. W. by S. ¾ S.	205¼	N. W. by W. ¾ W.	295¼
N. E. by N. ½ N.	28	S. E. by E. ½ E.	118	S. W. by S. ½ S.	208	N. W. by W. ½ W.	298
N. E. by N. ¼ N.	31	S. E. by E. ¼ E.	121	S. W. by S. ¼ S.	211	N. W. by W. ¼ W.	301
N. E. by N.	33¾	S. E. by E.	123¾	S. W. by S.	213¾	N. W. by W.	303¾
N. E. ¾ N.	36½	S. E. ¾ E.	126½	S. W. ¾ S.	216½	N. W. ¾ W.	306½
N. E. ½ N.	39½	S. E. ½ E.	129½	S. W. ½ S.	219½	N. W. ½ W.	309½
N. E. ¼ N.	42	S. E. ¼ E.	132¼	S. W. ¼ S.	222¼	N. W. ¼ W.	312¼
N. E.	45	S. E.	135	S. W.	225	N. W.	315
N. E. ¼ E.	47¾	S. E. ¼ S.	137¾	S. W. ¼ W.	227¾	N. W. ¼ N.	317¾
N. E. ½ E.	50½	S. E. ½ S.	140½	S. W. ½ W.	230½	N. W. ½ N.	320½
N. E. ¾ E.	53½	S. E. ¾ S.	143½	S. W. ¾ W.	233½	N. W. ¾ N.	323½
N. E. by E.	56¼	S. E. by S.	146¼	S. W. by W.	236¼	N. W. by N.	326¼
N. E. by E. ¼ E.	59	S. E. by S. ¼ S.	149	S. W. by W. ¼ W.	239	N. W. by N. ¼ N.	329
N. E. by E. ½ E.	62	S. E. by S. ½ S.	152	S. W. by W. ½ W.	242	N. W. by N. ½ N.	332
N. E. by E. ¾ E.	64¾	S. E. by S. ¾ S.	154¾	S. W. by W. ¾ W.	244¾	N. W. by N. ¾ N.	334¾
E. N. E.	67½	S. S. E.	157½	W. S. W.	247½	N. N. W.	337½
E. by N. ¾ N.	70¼	S. by E. ¾ E.	160¼	W. by S. ¾ S.	250¼	N. by W. ¾ W.	340¼
E. by N. ½ N.	73	S. by E. ½ E.	163	W. by S. ½ S.	253	N. by W. ½ W.	343
E. by N. ¼ N.	75	S. by E. ¼ E.	166	W. by S. ¼ S.	256	N. by W. ¼ W.	346
E. by N.	78¾	S. by E.	168¾	W. by S.	258¾	N. by W.	348¾
E. ¾ N.	81½	S. ¾ E.	171½	W. ¾ S.	261½	N. ¾ W.	351½
E. ½ N.	84½	S. ½ E.	174½	W. ½ S.	264½	N. ½ W.	854½
E. ¼ N.	87	S. ¼ E.	177¼	W. ¼ S.	267¼	N. ¼ W.	357¼
East	90	South	180	West	270	North	360

Converting compass points to degrees, and vice versa. (*From* Eldridge Tide and Pilot Book, 1984 *edition*) in the helmsman's eyes is ideal. A pure red light does not affect the eyes' night vision, and a very dim light just sufficient to show the pattern of the card will not have a hypnotic effect on the helmsman.

Next, consider what kind of card you want. Most modern yacht compasses are labeled in 30-degree intervals with 10- and 5-degree intervals indicated by longer and shorter radial marks. This is usually sufficient, for few indeed are the helmsmen who can steer a small boat closer than 2 degrees, an interval easily estimated between 5-degree graduations. A four-inch card graduated in 1- or 2-degree intervals can turn the helmsman dizzy and exhaust him in half an hour. Some old-timers, however, still prefer the card marked in points. This has advantages, once one has learned to "box the compass" and become familiar with the pattern of the card. Consider the quadrant from north to east. North and east are clearly marked with a big triangle and an E at east and with a distinctive design and an N at north. Northeast is also a big triangle and is labeled NE. Notice that northeast, halfway between north and east, combines their names. Halfway between north and northeast is a big diamond at north northeast, again a combination of the names of the two points between which it stands. The same is true of the big diamond at east northeast, halfway between east and northeast. To continue this system, however, would be cumbersome; the point east of north, between north and north northeast, is north by east. If you consider "by" to mean "1 point," the point is properly named "north one point east." Similarly, east by north is one point north of east. The point next north of northeast, between northeast and north northeast, is northeast by north, and the point east of northeast is northeast by east. One might call these points north northeast by east and east northeast by north, but convention decrees that after a point designated by three letters, nothing ever follows. The "by" points are indicated by smaller triangles and are unlettered.

We have now divided the quadrant into eight divisions,

each containing 11¼ degrees, and each point has been given a name that cannot be confused with the name of any other point, even when shouted to the helmsman on a rough and windy night. Also, we have marked the card in a clear and distinctive pattern in which each point has its obvious place, even when the compass is seen from a considerable distance and at an odd angle.

Should one want a more precise measurement than 11¼ degrees, each point is divided into halves and quarters. These are named from the points adjacent to them, always avoiding anything after a three-letter point. Thus, in boxing the compass by quarter points, one says:

North
N ¼ E
N ½ E
N ¾ E
N by E

N by E ¼ E
N by E ½ E
N by E ¾ E
NNE

NE by N ¾ N
NE by N ½ N
NE by N ¼ N
NE by N

NE ¾ N
NE ½ N
NE ¼ N
NE

The whole pattern unwinds again down to east. Thus the quadrant is divided into 32 divisions of 2.8 degrees each, certainly as close as anyone can steer. Each of the other quadrants maintains the same logical pattern.

The old man's objections to the modern card are based partly on nostalgia and partly on experience. The numbers are more easily confused than the points. For example, 260° and 280°, being each 10 degrees from west, are more easily confused both in hearing and in steering than west by south and west by north. Also, at least until one has become thoroughly familiar with the numbers, a bearing of 319° has little significance, whereas northwest by north is very clearly one point north of northwest with no mental arithmetic necessary.

On the other hand, the *Nautical Almanac* and all the sight reduction tables are tabulated in degrees. Therefore, all the plotting of position, dead reckoning, running fixes, and azimuths of celestial bodies must be calculated in degrees. A compass card without graduations in degrees means frequent reference to a conversion table and *another* chance to make a mistake.

Choose the card you like; one skipper friend of mine uses points for coastal work and orders to the helmsman, and degrees for celestial work. His compass is graduated in both. This also helps guests who know how to count to 360 but can't box the compass.

Another decision to be made is whether to include built-in correction magnets or to use external magnets. Perhaps the most satisfactory answer will come from your compass adjustor.

Ask about the bearing on which the card pivots. The best bearing is an industrial sapphire, which has very little friction and a long life. Less expensive instruments use hard plastic bearings.

Ask, too, whether the compass can be taken apart. Some are permanently sealed. If one of these develops a bubble, if the card or the dome darkens with age, or if the bearing wears, the compass must be replaced. One that can be taken apart can be repaired.

The material of which the sphere is made is important too. Most are now made of acrylic plastic, which is clearer than glass, darkens only very slowly if at all in sunlight, and is reasonably hard and scratch-resistant. Some are made of Lexan, a very hard, strong plastic used for football helmets and hockey masks. A compass dome made of Lexan has survived a point-blank shot from a .45. If the sphere is filled with oil, however, a Lexan dome will slowly darken from the inside and may be darkened from the outside by hydrocarbon pollutants in the air of a city anchorage.

You won't find out much about the liquid in which the card floats. The exact composition of this is considered a trade secret and manufacturers go about sniffing covertly at the bungholes of each other's compasses.

Compass Mounting

Consider next how your compass is to be mounted. In a powerboat, it is usually permanently mounted on a shelf in front of the principal steering station, where it will be protected from the weather and easily visible to the helmsman. It is important to see that control rods, steering cables, electrical wires, and electronic components such as radar scanners and display units—indeed all items with magnetic characteristics—are kept well away from it. Also, the compass should be so located that bearings can be taken across it from any direction. If this is impossible, another compass properly corrected should be installed on the flying bridge, or a hand bearing compass should be carried and a place found for it free of deviation.

On a sailing yacht, because the compass is so important an instrument and is thought of as the focal point of the vessel, it is usually installed in a binnacle in the middle of the cockpit. Here it is easily seen by the helmsman at the wheel, and it is in a convenient place from which to take bearings if the cabinhouse and the hood over the hatch are not too high. There are a few considerations to keep in mind, however, if the compass is to be so mounted. First, the binnacle must be very firmly bolted to the cockpit floor. People sitting in the cockpit have an almost irresistible tendency to brace themselves against the binnacle or to use it to pull themselves up. A heavy man thrown off balance to windward by an unexpected sea can fall against the binnacle with tremendous force. Second, the binnacle must be completely nonmagnetic. If the wheel is part of it, as is frequently the case, all the steering gear, especially the moving parts, must have nonmagnetic properties.

Usually a centrally mounted engine lies directly under the cockpit floor, often only a few feet from the compass. Engine vibration may shorten the life of the compass pivot bearing, and electrical fields set up by the alternator and associated wiring will affect the compass differently under sail and power. A steel exhaust pipe running close to the compass, alternately hot and cold, may even change its magnetic properties from time to time. A brass exhaust pipe will solve this problem.

One offshore racing yawl on which I sailed had a standard compass mounted on top of the cabinhouse, firmly bolted down and protected by bronze rails. Two smaller compasses, one on each side, were mounted within easy view of the helmsman sitting either to port or starboard. The course was set by the standard compass, which was as far as possible from the steel hull, was easily visible to the navigator from the hatch, and afforded a clear view all around the horizon for taking bearings. The helmsman could see the standard compass when he stood up and could steer comfortably by one of the others.

Bracket mounting may absorb some of the engine vibration in the bracket and also makes it possible to stow the compass below when it is not being used, thus protecting it from the careless guest and the light-fingered prowler. If the boat is steered with a tiller, an off-center mounting is to be preferred, since a parallax of several degrees can be caused by looking at the compass from the side. Brackets installed on either side of the cockpit allow the compass to be shifted according to the helmsman's position, but this system is no solution at all unless the compass is compensated for both sides. If one side must be chosen, probably the starboard side is best. Most people are right-eyed, and on the starboard side would have the right eye forward. Under power, a vessel approaching from the starboard side has the right of way, so it is wise to give the helmsman an unobstructed view to starboard. Under sail, of course, a helmsman on the port tack would probably be sitting to port with a poor view of the compass *and* of an approaching right-of-way vessel on the starboard tack. If he sat to leeward, he couldn't see to windward and his vision to leeward would be obstructed by the genoa jib. But at least he could see the compass.

Other installations are possible. Commercial sailing vessels and fishermen used to install the compass behind a window in the after side of the house, where it could be well protected and easily lighted. Some yachts set the compass into the after side of the house and some set it under the deck, forward of the helm and to one side. Here it is well protected, but the glass or plastic deadlight over it soon becomes scratched and clouded, and it is a difficult place from which to take bearings.

The owner must adopt an installation convenient to his own boat and his own preferences as a helmsman and navigator, but in any case he should provide for a firm and well-protected installation away from immediate magnetic and electrical influences.

Compass Compensation

Finally, the compass should be properly compensated. One can do nothing about variation, which is the error introduced by the difference between the magnetic pole of the earth (toward which the compass points) and the geographic pole (the center of the earth's rotation). Over a period of years the error changes insignificantly, and by using the inner or magnetic rose on the chart, allowance is made for it automatically.

Deviation, on the other hand, can be largely compensated for. This is error induced by magnetic influences aboard the vessel. An iron keel, an engine, a steel fuel tank, or an iron stove near the compass will cause a large and obvious error. These errors change with the heading of the boat as their influence operates at different angles to the earth's magnetic field, but they can be compensated for more or less permanently. There are also other, more subtle and variable causes of deviation. Cast iron ballast (sash weights, for instance) may sometimes change magnetic characteristics for no apparent reason. Soft iron, if heated or hammered, and especially if held vertically, will assume magnetic properties and change them with change of position. A steel backstay, especially a running backstay, can affect the compass. A life raft near the compass on my boat once threw it off badly when inadvertently turned end for end, bringing the steel pressure cylinder closer to the compass.

Then there are minor and even more temporary causes of deviation. A bucket left in the cockpit can cause error. Canned goods stowed in a cockpit locker or a knife left in the binnacle may set you ashore. One foggy summer afternoon I found myself badly confused. None of my courses seemed to be coming out right. Finally I noticed that one of my guests had a camera bag near the compass, in which was an exposure meter containing a powerful little magnet. A magnetic knife rack, door catch, chess game, or child's toy may upset the compass badly. A fisherman leaving the harbor one night set his portable radio near the compass and fetched up high and dry on a ledge. The influence of a magnet or a piece of steel is inversely proportional to the square of its distance from the compass, so all that is necessary is to clear the area within about four feet of the binnacle, except, of course, for such massive pieces of iron as a keel or an engine.

With the compass in its permanent position and all magnetic influences either permanently established or removed as far as possible from the compass, it should now be professionally compensated. It is possible, of course, to make a deviation table to avoid the trouble and expense of compensation. This involves running as many charted courses as possible on a clear day and plotting the errors on a graph. Theoretically this is not a difficult task, but practically it is not so simple. A great number of different courses must be sailed, and they must be distributed widely around the compass, say every 15 degrees. Each course must be steered long enough to let the compass settle down and to allow for the vagaries of the helmsman. If one uses government buoys for marks, the courses chosen must be long courses, for buoys are not always located precisely as charted and a short course may introduce a significant error. Shown here is a deviation chart constructed as carefully as it could be done in one

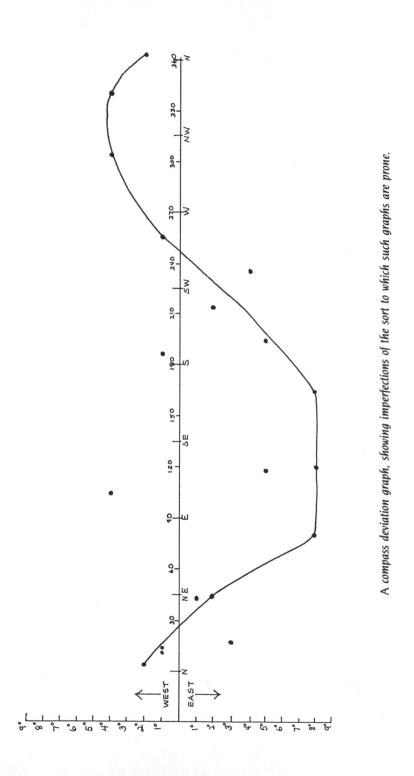

A compass deviation graph, showing imperfections of the sort to which such graphs are prone.

day. The reader will see at once that the curve, which was drawn as close to as many points on the graph as possible, has had to bypass several points, assuming that because they are inconsistent with other observations they are in error. That may not be the case. Also, suspicion may be aroused by the lack of symmetry of the curve and by the unusually flat part between east and southeast. One might wonder why the error at south is not the reverse of the error at north, or at least close to the reverse—and the same doubt may arise for east and west. In short, the navigator, with all the variables he already has to contend with, may be very reluctant to have to regard his compass as another dubious variable. In my opinion, the best solution is to employ a competent professional compass adjustor to do the job with an azimuth, an instrument for taking an accurate bearing of the sun.

On a quiet sunny day, the compass adjustor will set up his instrument in your cockpit, meticulously orienting it fore and aft. From the *Nautical Almanac* and the sight reduction tables he will have drawn a chart showing the precise magnetic bearing of the sun for the date, time, and position. He will then ask the helmsman to steer north by the ship's compass. By adjusting the built-in magnet or by taping a magnet to the side of the binnacle, he will compensate for error on a northerly course. He will then have the helmsman steer east and will compensate for the error on this course. There should be no deviation on a southerly heading, but if he finds a few degrees of deviation, he will move the magnet to compensate for half of it, thus introducing (of course) an equal deviation on a northerly course. The same process is followed for east and west. If it appears that on all courses there is a deviation in the same direction—to starboard, for instance—the errors are averaged and the compass turned in the binnacle to port to compensate for the average error. This should leave almost no deviation. After checking for possible error on intercardinal points, the adjustor will leave you with a deviation card showing what minor errors he was unable to remove and with the confidence that your compass indeed points north. In most wooden, aluminum, or fiberglass yachts, errors can be completely eliminated or at worst diminished to a very few degrees of deviation on a few courses, usually so few that only the most skillful helmsman could steer within such a tolerance.

Of course, you can perform this operation for yourself in a variety of ways. You can set up ranges on north-south and east-west courses if they can be precisely established. One yachtsman used weighted buoys, dropping one, steering north, dropping the other, heading back for the first and halving the error between south and his course to the buoy, and so on. Another used a square of 2 x 6 with a pencil set up vertically in the center. He aligned it fore and aft and steered so the shadow of the sun fell on one corner. He then steered so the shadow fell on the opposite corner, halved the error, and so on. All of these ingenious methods introduce errors. The helmsman may not line up the ranges quite accurately, or the current may set the vessel off. Buoys drift, the sun moves, and human error creeps in at unsuspected mouseholes. Granted that a professional adjustor may introduce errors, too, but they are likely to be smaller.

Even the most arrogant and precise student of the compass will admit that compass compensation is at best an inexact science, and the skipper must be ever on the alert for new sources of error. In the course of a cruise, he should seize every opportunity to check the accuracy of his compass by running courses and by taking occasional cross bearings. One yachtsman performing such an exercise found that his compass course was taking him over the top of a very solid piece of Maine real estate. He called in the man who had adjusted the compass only shortly before, and they found no error when checking the instrument carefully under power on a quiet day. On the day on which the error had been found, however, the vessel was sailing well heeled. The change in angle had caused changes in the horizontal distance from the compass of the compensating magnets and of the iron that had introduced the deviation in the first place. It is possible to compensate for heeling error by installing a magnet directly under the center of the compass, but this is seldom done. It is a very fussy correction. Since the error changes with the ship's latitude and is usually quite small in any case, correction is worth considering only when the vessel will be heeled consistently for a considerable time. Nevertheless, the navigator must be alert to this possibility as well as to manifold other possibilities of error.

Steel vessels obviously have considerable compass error. Much of this is induced when the vessel is built. Iron or steel, if heated, bent, or hammered, will pick up magnetism. The amount and direction of this will depend partly on the direction in which the vessel lies in the building yard and partly on the composition of the metal and the amount of violence to which it is subjected in the building process. After the vessel is launched and has been used for a season or two, this magnetism settles down to a consistent amount and direction and allows accurate compass compensation.

With a good compass properly installed and compensated, and with an observant and fussy navigator at the chart table, we are ready to consider what other navigational equipment to put aboard.

3

Charts and Other Publications

Late one lovely summer afternoon over a quarter century ago, I anchored in Tenant's Harbor, Maine, ahead of a handsome blue Alden schooner. After we had snugged down and finished dinner, we were hailed by the skipper of the schooner, who asked, "How do I get to Bar Harbor from here?"

I started to tell him, but it was clear that he was unfamiliar with the Fox Islands Thorofare and Eggemoggin Reach, and that he had never heard of Merchant Row. He invited me aboard. He was a cheerful fellow, a dentist. He asked his wife to pass up two cans of beer.

"How can you drink beer at a time like this?" she asked.

"Madame," he replied, "the oral orifice of man is so constructed that it will fit over a triangular opening, and that is how I can drink beer now or any other time."

After this introduction, I suggested that he pull out the charts of Penobscot and Blue Hill bays. He looked mystified—never heard of them. From his hip pocket he produced a map printed on the back of a bus timetable, which he had used to navigate east from a Massachusetts port.

This story I have heard repeated in different and even more picturesque settings so many times that I am convinced a special Providence watches over the ignorant. The rest of us, however, are expected to take care of ourselves.

Obtaining Charts

First you will want a small-scale National Ocean Survey chart (about 1:400,000) covering the whole area of your contemplated cruise, principally as a guide to laying out and subsequently modifying your long-range plans. The National Ocean Survey also covers the coasts on a 1:80,000 scale, about an inch to the nautical mile. These charts of course show much greater detail than the planning charts, but lack soundings in many harbors, bays, and passages and do not show all buoys. The 1:40,000 scale charts are almost incredibly accurate. The navigator should supply himself with a full set of these and with such of the 1:20,000 scale charts as are pertinent to his cruise. These are not only more detailed, but the larger scale makes intricate passages more clear.

If the navigator is new to his job, he should provide himself with the most recently issued National Ocean Survey Chart Number 1, which gives the meaning of all abbreviations and explains graphically the new color codes and light characteristics that have been adopted to conform to international patterns.

Charts may be purchased by mail directly from the Distribution Branch N/CG33, National Ocean Service, 6501 Lafayette Avenue, Riverdale, Maryland 20737. Charts are also available at retail outlets in most coastal cities and many coastal towns. However, it is well to buy a full set before sailing day since local sources, especially late in the season, are likely to have every chart except the one you lack.

It is best to order charts by number and title to be sure of getting the right ones. A chart catalog is available from the National Ocean Survey or from any chart outlet.

United States charts are exceptionally accurate. The large-scale ones show in detail every rock and ledge, every little nubbin, bump, and outcrop on the shores. They also show contours both above and below the surface and, of course, they show frequent soundings. The mariner who reports indignantly that he struck an uncharted rock is more likely to have struck an unnoticed rock. Accurate as they are, however, charts must be used with some caution. For instance, where the bottom is sandy and subject to swift currents and heavy seas, the sand may drift like snow during a storm and leave a shoal where there was deep water a week ago. Buoys are sometimes not found exactly where the chart says they should be, either because the Coast Guard in replacing a buoy made a small error or because for one reason or another, such as storm or collision, the buoy has shifted or even gone adrift. Automated lights occasionally get out of adjustment, fog signals on unmanned stations are not always started when the mariner most needs them, and soundings are at best approximate. Within very narrow tolerances, however, the chart is the navigator's most reliable source of information.

To accumulate and print all the information on a chart is extremely expensive. The United States government seems to have abandoned the notion that providing accurate and up-to-date charts is a government responsibility, so charts are no longer corrected to the date of sale but rather are sold as printed. Also, in accordance with the belief that those who use the charts should pay for them, the price of charts is escalating rapidly. It is neither practically nor financially possible to buy a full set of accurate charts before every cruise. Therefore one must keep his charts up to date himself. The Coast Guard prints a *Notice to Mariners* weekly and mails it free to anyone interested. Write your local Coast Guard district office to get on the subscription list.

To make weekly corrections on your charts throughout the year in order to have them correct on sailing day is something of a nuisance. At a price, there are shortcuts. One is to purchase annually the *Light and Buoy List* (CG–158) from the Superintendent of Documents, U.S. Government Printing Office, Washington, D.C. 20402. It is also available at many chart outlets. This list is correct as of the date when it goes to press in December. Shortly after it is issued in the spring, the local *Notice to Mariners* prints a list of corrections to date. You will have to make corrections from subsequent issues of the *Notice to Mariners* from then on. Then the Light List can be compared to the chart you are actually using. Inasmuch as the rocks and ledges are rather permanent, changes to the charts are made only in the lights and buoys. Check the buoy for which you are running on the chart against the updated Light List to see if it is still there, is still the same color, and still shows the same light characteristics.

Another alternative is the Better Boating Association's *Chart Kits*. These are large, spiral-bound books, about 17 inches by 22 inches, or a fourth the size of a chart. Each book includes parts of a great many charts, some enlarged and some reduced. In 1985 there were eleven volumes covering the coasts from Maine to the west coast of Florida, the southern California coast to Point Conception, Lake Michigan, and parts of the Bahamas and Virgin Islands. With the appropriate volume you can cover any cruising area quite well. Furthermore, these charts are republished and brought up to date about every two years. Every year the Better Boating Association publishes a booklet of relevant excerpts from *Notice to Mariners*, from which the charts in your book may be corrected. If you would prefer to use your own NOS charts, which are larger and in some cases more convenient, you can correct your own charts from the *Chart Kit*. With *Notice to Mariners* free, the Light List at $11.00 in 1984, and the *Chart Kit* at $65.00, you can keep your charts current at prices inversely proportional to the hours you wish to put into the project.

Working with Charts

Charts are best kept flat. Ideally a chart should not be folded, for it seems that by some corollary of Murphy's Law one's course frequently runs across a badly worn crease, and occasionally a vital buoy or sounding is located where the creases intersect. However, few indeed are the small boats with space enough for a drawer three feet by four. Rolled charts have no creases but are fiendishly hard to handle and if carried on deck must be folded anyway. Most yachts carry their charts folded two ways. They can be stowed under a bunk cushion quite conveniently. Each should be labeled in large letters both by number and title on the same corner, and the set should be kept in geographical order.

Most large ocean cruising and racing yachts have a navigator's "office" with chart table, desk, book shelf, and an array of instruments. Lacking this, the small boat navigator should try to arrange his cabin so that he has a chart table: a flat surface at least one-quarter as big as a chart, say 1½ feet by 2 feet, but the bigger the better. While you can use the regular cabin table, navigation must be suspended during meals or meals deferred during fog runs. One vessel on which I served as navigator had as its only available surface the top of the ice box, requiring removal of the chart whenever thirst overcame one of the crew, an event which occurred with distressing frequency. On my boat, a piece of plywood hinged to the forward side of the after cabin bulkhead can be lowered when needed for a chart table but hooked up out of the way at other times.

Near the chart table should be a few tools, particularly dividers and parallel rules or a protractor. Many people prefer the brass dividers with a ring at the top, which can be manipulated with one hand. These are expensive and the steel points rust quickly. A bit of fine sandpaper and a drop of oil will keep them clean. Parallel rules are simple, and once one gets the knack of walking them across the chart, they are easy to use and quick. Furthermore, they allow bearings to be easily and accurately reversed by simply reading the opposite side of the compass rose. However, they do require a flat surface. A plastic protractor can bend over slight irregularities, but each course plotted requires two readings, one to line up the protractor with the compass rose and one to read the course—two chances to make a mistake.

There are several patented course plotters on the market, most of which clamp to the chart table, can be aligned with the compass rose, and require only that the straightedge be laid along the course and the bearing read off. The simplest arrangement made is a transparent plastic sheet with parallel lines about ¼ inch apart. If one line is laid along your course, another is certain to be found very close indeed to the center of the compass rose.

A generous supply of pencils, erasers, and scratch paper should be at hand.

Other Publications

Besides charts and the Light List, it is well to have a copy of the current *Coast Pilot*, which is available at chart outlets or from the National Ocean Service. This is republished by the government annually in January or February and can be corrected from *Notice to Mariners*. It describes many of the ledges, islands, and navigational aids, gives suggested routes, and lists facilities available at different ports, such as fuel wharves, marine railways, and supply stores. The introduction and appendixes contain a wealth of interesting information on weather, bridges, and laws governing the navigation of large vessels—thus making their movements more predictable to yachtsmen.

The Eldridge Tide and Pilot Book, published annually by Robert E. White, 64 Commercial Wharf, Boston, Massachusetts 02110, has a wealth of information for East Coast mariners. Of particular importance are tide tables and tidal current information for many points from Isle au Haut, Maine, to Miami. Current charts for each hour of the tide cover the area between New York and Boston. The principal lights and fog signals between the Strait of Canso in Nova Scotia and the Dry Tortugas are listed with their characteristics, including lights on Bermuda. Also included are a few astronomical tables; information on radiobeacons, Loran, VHF radio, and weather; and fascinating miscellaneous information on topics such as the Beaufort scale and when to fly the national ensign.

Cruising guides, privately published, have been written for most popular cruising areas. They differ widely in their quality and the extent of their detail, but most of them are written by small boat sailors for yachtsmen. They give useful local information: "On a southerly breeze the horn on the light is inaudible a mile to windward but can be heard clearly for miles to leeward." Or: "Note that this buoy is to be left to starboard as it is a mark for the coastal channel and not for entrance to the harbor. Give it a good berth on rounding it, for the ledge it marks extends far to the east." They also furnish directions for entering harbors: "Steer for the cottage with the blue roof until . . . ." Advice on where to anchor, where to land, depth alongside, location of yacht clubs, telephones, bus service, grocery stores, and repair services is given. Sometimes there is also interesting historical information, suggestions about what to see and do ashore, and a lot of general and miscellaneous information. Unfortunately these books are expensive, and they can be rewritten only at intervals of about five years, so the cottage with the blue roof may now have a red roof and a condominium may have taken the place of the boatyard. Much of the information will be good, however, and the author will be grateful for a letter describing changes.

A logbook is not exactly a publication, but it can be even more valuable. Various logbooks are published with ruled columns for engine revolutions, barometer readings, and fuel supply cluttering the pages. A hardbound blank notebook such as law students use is to be preferred. For fog navigation you should note at the top of the page the date, the time of high water, and the wind conditions. For each course sailed you should note, in the same order for each course, the time of departure, the course, the speed, and the distance to the next mark. Add as you go along every bit of possibly pertinent information such as changes in depth of water, observation of current flowing by a buoy or lobster trap, sound of gulls on a distant ledge, rumble of surf, passing vessels, anything that can help. If you fail to make your mark, a careful review of your log may suggest in which direction you were set off. After you get straightened out, a review of the log with chart and parallel rule will show just what happened and will help you to plot a successful course the next time you make that passage. Chapter 8 contains such an exercise. Also, in case of accident a logbook that has been kept accurately and consistently is acceptable as legal evidence of what happened.

It is also very much worthwhile to record matters of general or personal interest, and particularly how you feel about each experience. This makes the log an interesting journal of your cruise, for times and distances mean nothing very much to the reader afterward, but the feeling of relief and satisfaction at the end of a successful fog run is worth remembering and savoring in later years.

4

Other Equipment

The Ship's Clock

After the compass, a clock is the most necessary instrument. Of course the navigator can use his wristwatch, but there is some advantage in having a reliable clock permanently fastened in clear view of the navigator, helmsman, cook, and everyone else. This clock should keep "ship's time," the official time by which watches are changed, meals are served, and the log kept. The clock may not be dead accurate, but at least everyone will know what time it is. It is the navigator's responsibility to see that the clock is wound regularly and that it is more or less in agreement with local time ashore. With this clock in view, he can log consistently his times of sighting buoys and his arrivals and departures; furthermore, in estimating the time at which a buoy should materialize out of the fog, he will not have to remember by which timepiece he made his calculations.

Speed Logs

The means of determining a vessel's speed through the water vary widely in accuracy, complexity, and expense. The simplest, cheapest, and not always the least accurate method is to guess. If you have sailed the boat for a number of seasons and have kept any kind of reckoning of times and distances, you can look over the side and make a good guess at how fast the water is going by. This is likely to be pretty reliable in a sailing vessel at near or slightly under hull speed. At higher speeds, the splash, wash, wake, noise, angle of heel, and exhilaration increase much more rapidly than actual speed, so one is likely to overestimate. At much slower speeds, a slight error in estimating the speed becomes a large percentage error in estimating the time required to sail a course. For instance, if you guess your speed at 1½ knots when it is only one knot, you will be 20 minutes late in making a mark a mile away. Twenty minutes is a *long* time in the fog!

The next cheapest method is the Dutchman's log. This consists in measuring off a given distance along the side of the boat, dropping a chip at the forward mark and timing the boat's progress by it. Suppose, for instance, we measure off 25 feet, drop a chip, and find it takes 3.7 seconds to sail that distance. Then, 6,080 (number of feet in a nautical mile) divided by 25 feet gives 243.2 blocks of 25 feet in a mile. If the boat travels one of those blocks in 3.7 seconds, it will take 243.2 times 3.7 seconds to travel a mile. So we travel a mile in 899.8 seconds. Divide by 60 to find the number of minutes it takes to travel a mile and we get 14.99, or 15 minutes for practical purposes. A mile in 15 minutes is four miles in an hour, so we are going four knots.

Of course it is not necessary to carry out all the arithmetic for each estimate of speed. It can be done once, plotted on a curve, and tacked over the chart table. From the sample curve shown here it is evident that at slow speeds, the

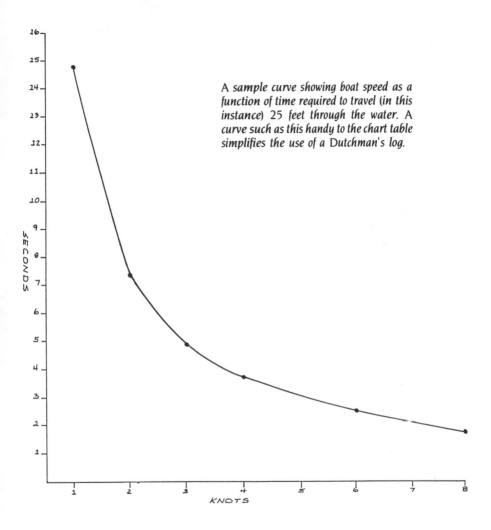

A sample curve showing boat speed as a function of time required to travel (in this instance) 25 feet through the water. A curve such as this handy to the chart table simplifies the use of a Dutchman's log.

method is fairly accurate, but to time the difference between 2.11 seconds for 7 knots and 1.87 seconds for 8 knots calls for a quick hand on the watch, a sharp eye on the chip, and a minimum of wash along the rail.

If your engine has a tachometer, a table of engine speed against boat speed can be quite reliable in calm water, but against a head wind and a steep head sea, it is at best a guide to guessing.

The next least expensive, the most accurate, but not the easiest method is the chip log. This was much used by old-time navigators in sail. Make a "chip"—that is, a pie-shaped piece of wood with a radius of about a foot—and weight it so it will float upright with the curved edge down. Bore a hole in each corner and attach the log line to the top hole. Then, by means of a wooden clothespin and a wedge, rig a bridle so the chip will float upright. The log line is wound on a reel that will turn freely. About 20 feet from the chip a white rag is tied into the line, and ten feet farther up the line a red rag. Beyond the red rag is a series of knots spaced according to the following plan.

If the vessel were to travel at one nautical mile per hour for an hour, the chip, floating stationary in the water, would draw out a mile of line, 6,080 feet. In half an hour it would draw out half that, 3,040 feet. In one minute it would draw out $6080/60 = 101.3$ feet. At eight knots it would draw eight times that, or 810.4 feet. Even that amount of line on a reel would be cumbersome, so, rather arbitrarily perhaps, the old-timers used a 14-second sandglass. The distance between knots can be calculated thus:

$$\frac{14 \text{ seconds}}{3600 \text{ seconds in an hour}} = \frac{x \text{ feet between knots}}{6080 \text{ feet in a mile}}$$

$$3600x = 85120$$

$$x = \frac{85120}{3600}$$

$$x = 23.6 \text{ feet}$$

Beyond the red rag, then, knots are tied every 23.6 feet for one more knot than you think the vessel can possibly sail.

Two people are needed to operate the chip log. One holds the sandglass or stopwatch. The other holds the chip and the reel. He drops the chip, which remains stationary in the water astern. When the white rag goes over the rail, he calls "Ready." When the red rag goes over, he calls "Mark" and the timer starts the watch. After ten seconds, the timer starts counting seconds aloud: "eleven . . . twelve

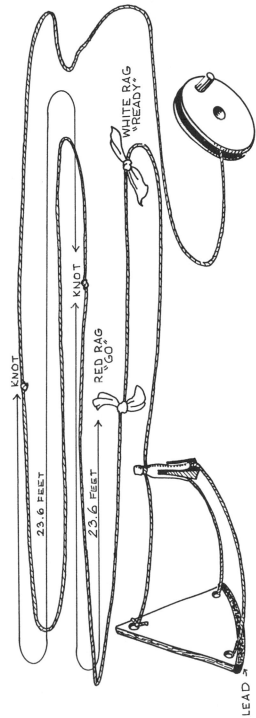

The chip log, an inexpensive and reliable speed-measuring device. Its use is described in the accompanying text.

KNOT

WHITE RAG
"READY"

KNOT

23.6 FEET

RED RAG
"GO"

23.6 FEET

LEAD

... thirteen ... STOP." The line is instantly stopped and the number of knots that have gone over the rail is counted and noted as the vessel's speed. Thus, six knots is six nautical miles per hour.

When the line is stopped, the wedge pulls out of the clothespin and the chip is easily hauled in as it planes along the surface.

There is a story that in the days of the hard-driving tea clippers the mate was holding the sandglass while a Chinese boy held the reel. The line ran out rapidly, reached its bitter end, and yanked the reel and its holder over the rail. The callous mate is reported to have written in the deck log, "Fine fair breeze. All sail set. Vessel going 14 knots and a Chinaman." The expression "going 14 knots and a Chinaman" became proverbial for a time but is seldom heard today.

The chip log is inexpensive, simple, and if carefully measured, accurate to a fraction of a knot at any speed. However, it is a little slow and cumbersome and takes two people.

The patent log was developed from the chip log. This is a woven line long enough to tow a rotor clear of the vessel's wake. The line is attached to an instrument that turns as the line twists, and converts the number of turns to distance through the water. The best ones, like the Walker log, are quite accurate, and as their small error is more or less constant, it can be allowed for. This log gives distance, which must be divided by time to get speed; but as distance is the factor we really want anyway, that is no problem. At slow speeds, however, there is not enough force in the twist of the line to overcome the instrument's inertia, and until the rotor has wound a number of turns into the line, the instrument does not register. Then the instrument spins madly until the turns have been taken out of the line, and then remains still again. At very slow speeds, the rotor may not turn at all.

The line must be handled carefully on being hauled in, because it will kink up into a horrible tangle unless hauled in over one side of the stern and passed overboard over the other to let it tow backward and take out the kinks.

Cheap patent logs with light flywheels are highly unreliable at almost any speed and even the best patent logs are useless when the rotor is clogged with weed or eaten by a passing shark. The patent log is not a solution recommended for coastal cruising in the fog, for it is expensive, inaccurate at slow speeds, and subject to failure.

There are numerous electrical and mechanical logs that register speed and sometimes distance on a dial. Some depend on a pitot tube, a vertical tube passed through the bottom of the boat and bent forward. Pressure proportional to the speed of the boat builds up in the tube and registers as speed on a dial. Other logs depend on a vane or wire through the bottom of the boat; the vane is pressed aft by the flow of water, the pressure being registered as speed on a dial. Another system uses a little waterwheel with four blades, each with a tiny magnet. As the water turns the blades, they pass by a coil and generate a current proportional to the speed of the boat. All of these instruments are expensive, but most of them are quite accurate if carefully calibrated by timing a run over a given distance in smooth water or by use of a chip log.

The principal difficulty with all of these logs lies in fouling with weed, floating logs, or lobster trap warps. The pitot tube and the vane are the worst offenders here. Although some are painted with antifoulant at the factory, anything immersed in salt water will be fouled by marine growth after a short time. Inspect the outboard part of the instrument occasionally and remove it and soak it for a few hours in Clorox to clean it easily, gently, and completely. It is better to clean a rotor frequently than to paint it with antifouling paint. The paint is almost certain to gum up the tiny plastic axle on which the blades spin.

There are other more sophisticated and more expensive ways of measuring speed, involving the transmission of sound or electric impulses between two points on the outside of the hull. These too, however, must be calibrated and are subject to distortion by marine growth if not by floating debris.

Depth Sounders

The compass, clock, and log determine course, time, and distance, the three significant factors necessary to keep run of one's position on the chart. However, another factor is very helpful to keep track of—the depth of water. The old-timers used a greased sounding lead with a marked line. This is still the simplest and cheapest way to determine the depth, but where other methods are available, the lead has serious drawbacks. First, the vessel must be stopped or radically slowed down. Second, the process is slow. In a depth of 10 fathoms, it takes a considerable time to get bottom and haul the line back. Third, it is a cold, wet job. Fourth, it takes considerable strength and skill to stand at the rail of a lively yacht, swing a seven-pound lead in a complete circle, release it just after the bottom of the swing, pay out the line without a hitch, and grab it in time to feel the bottom. If the lead in descending from the top of the swing should hit the deck, the scar would be permanent. Finally, the lead is not very accurate, due to the sag of the line as the lead sinks. Despite colorful tales of fishermen navigating from bank to bank by the depth and character of the bottom, the "blue pigeon" is not a good modern way of determining depth.

The answer is the depth finder. This machine emits a sound wave and measures the time it takes to bounce off the bottom and return. It then displays the depth on a dial, a digital scale, a video screen, or a tracing on a revolving drum. The first two types are the least expensive. The video screen shows the contour of the bottom over which you have recently traveled. The paper tracing can be kept as a permanent record and compared with tracings from subsequent trips over the same route to give an idea of your position.

In purchasing any kind of depth finder for a cruising boat, it is well to get one that will show depths down to 300 feet. A study of the chart will show that one's position may often be clearly indicated by a sudden change in depth. For instance, off the Maine coast, just south of the Cape Porpoise whistle on the course from York whistle, are several peaks that rise to about 100 feet from 150 feet or more. Also, one can often navigate safely along a jagged coastline by following the 20 fathom contour. Off Cutler, Maine, the 100-foot contour will lead you right to the bell at the entrance to the harbor.

It is important to keep the depth sounder's transducer clean. Some types cannot be painted without interfering with their efficiency. Others can. In either case, marine growth will eventually foul a transducer and must be gently wiped off. Rough treatment will gouge the plastic face and permanently distort the signal.

The signal can also be distorted or even nullified if the vessel is heeled consistently or is sailing hard into a steep chop, driving air bubbles under her hull and past the transducer. Sometimes one must heave to, or at least slow down, to get a reliable sounding. An expensive alternative is to install a second transducer on the other side of the boat, with a gravity switch that will activate the lower one.

5

Electronic
Aids

Radio Direction Finders

The manually operated radio direction finder provides a useful check on one's position. It is simply a radio with a loop antenna. When the loop is at right angles to the radio waves to which the set is tuned, the signal is the loudest; conversely, when the loop lies parallel to the incoming waves, the signal will be faintest. A number of coastal radio beacons with ranges of 5 to 100 miles broadcast characteristic signals on 272 to 322 kHz at intervals stated in the Light List and in Eldridge. Theoretically, one can tune to a station, rotate the loop until a null or low point in sound is found, record the bearing, and plot it on the chart. A second bearing should pinpoint the vessel's position. However, it is not that neat. First, over any considerable distance radio waves diverge, so that the null may be quite wide on a distant station. Furthermore, radio waves are refracted by passing over land; usually this creates only a minor error but one serving at least to widen the null.

Radio waves also make no allowance for the curvature of the earth but travel on great circle courses. An allowance must therefore be made when plotting long-range bearings on a Mercator chart. There is a table in the Appendix to the *Coast Pilot* giving these corrections.

Finally, errors are introduced by steel rigging and other metal in the boat. These can be determined and allowed for. With the set in its permanent position and its lubber line oriented to the vessel's head, select a buoy a mile or more from a radio direction finding station but in sight of it. Sail by the buoy on courses every 15 degrees around the compass, taking the RDF bearing of the station each time the buoy lines up with the station. Plot the errors just as you would plot compass deviations. It is a tedious business, but makes your RDF far more useful.

Enclosing the set in a closed loop may make it inoperative. On one vessel I found that the RDF would not receive at all until the gate in the lifeline was opened. On some vessels a vertical closed loop is formed by the rigging, and if a shroud touches a lifeline, two intersecting loops may be formed.

If a handheld RDF is used, especially one with a compass, the problem is slightly different. First a place on the vessel must be found where there is no deviation. Head the vessel for a distant mark, noting the course by chart and by the standard steering compass. Then try various places on deck until you find one where the compass on the RDF reads the same as the standard compass. Try this with several different courses until you find the magic spot. On wooden, aluminum, or fiberglass yachts, it will often be on the foredeck or way aft on the counter. Once the magic spot is found, run a few courses near a station to be sure rigging or deck structures do not interfere with radio waves. Your RDF may now be of considerable help.

If you want a more sophisticated instrument, you can buy an automatic direction finder, known as an ADF. This is permanently installed, with a fixed, double-loop antenna.

It tunes itself accurately to the source of the radio signal and shows the bearing automatically on a scale. It is more sensitive to distant stations and more accurate than the manually operated portable or handheld sets, but it must be installed and adjusted by an electronics expert and is much more expensive than either the portable or the handheld model.

An RDF is most useful if you are running directly for the transmitting station, homing in on it. As you approach, the signal becomes stronger and the null narrower. If you are set off course significantly by wind or current, the RDF will tell you. It is also useful in passing a station, for as you go by, the signal slowly draws aft and gives reasonable assurance of position. It is least useful when used to take a cross bearing on two stations, for the spread in both nulls compounds the errors, although RDFs with digital nulls reduce the spreads. The instrument can also be used on commercial radio stations, usually much more powerful than stations on lighthouses. Any radio station will give you the latitude and longitude of its transmitter on request. However, these transmitters are often well inland and off your chart.

With all its imperfections, the RDF can still be very helpful, and no source of information is so useless as to be neglected by the careful navigator.

Loran

Loran C is an extremely sophisticated navigational system. When it is properly used and in good working order, it comes close to eliminating entirely the uncertainty of navigating in the fog. The theory is simple. Suppose two radio stations, A and B, broadcast signals simultaneously. If a vessel receives the two signals simultaneously, it is equidistant from A and B on a perpendicular bisector of the line connecting them. This bisector is a "line of position." Now introduce another station, C, timed to send a signal at the same instant as the other two. If the signals from A and C arrive at the same time, then the vessel is on a line of position perpendicular to line AC, and hence it is at the intersection of the two lines of position. In practice, complications unimaginable to the clock-and-compass navigator must be introduced. The signals must not actually be sent simultaneously or the receiver will confuse them. Furthermore, lines of position other than that on the bisector of the base line are not straight lines but hyperbolic curves. Finally, the time differences are measured in *millionths* of a second. Inside the set is a computer, which unscrambles these signals and supplies the navigator with his position either in terms of time differences or of latitude and longitude. The computer also gives him a wealth of other information, such as course and distance to his destination and an estimated time of arrival, way points, course made good over the bottom, and even others.

As in the much simpler case of the radio direction finder, however, there are numerous possible sources of difficulty. The electronic problems are the most easily solved. The antenna must be clear of electronic interference, and the ground and power supply must be adequate. There must be a minimum of interference from generators, alternators, and other electronic equipment on the vessel. The receiver must be kept clean and dry, and all connections must be bright and tight.

Besides electronic problems, there may also be interference with the signal either through malfunction of the station sending the signal or through interference caused by other radio transmitters, thunderstorms, weather fronts, or the nature of the land over which the signal passes.

The most serious source of error, however, is the operator himself. He must practice with the instrument constantly, know what information it can supply, how to elicit that information, of what aberrations to be suspicious, and the nature and extent of possible errors. The navigator should note on a clear day the position given by his set as he passes any significant point to which he is likely to return in the fog. The set may reflect a slight error—sometimes a considerable one—but it will reflect the same error at that place every time, so if the reading at the Cross Rip horn buoy, for instance, is noted on a clear day, the navigator can return to those coordinates in the fog at night. Even if he cannot see the buoy, he can reach out his hand and touch it. The precision of a Loran in good order is incredible.

Radar

Radar appears to the prospective purchaser to be the answer to prayer. It opens a window through which he can see through fog and darkness. But should he look into the scope on a vessel with a set in operation, he would realize that to make it truly useful takes much thought and practice.

If he is really serious about installing a radar set, he must consider carefully its location. The scanner is highly magnetic. It should be located at least six feet from the compass, and before being permanently bolted down, it should be revolved by hand with the boat on several different headings to be sure that no deviation is being introduced. If a magnetic autopilot is used, that too should be checked out lest it switch from port helm to starboard at every revolution of the magnetron. If a spare magnetron is carried, it should be stowed in the same place at all times; and if it is used, the old one should not be hove overboard but should be stowed in the place of the spare. Also, the scanner must be located where it can be easily reached for servicing, yet high enough on the vessel so it will have a clear "view" all around the horizon. A lifeboat, a deck structure, an exhaust stack, or a mast will create a blind spot on the scope. On many sailing vessels, the mast is the only feasible location, but one must remember that the scanner weighs fifty to one hundred pounds, and located

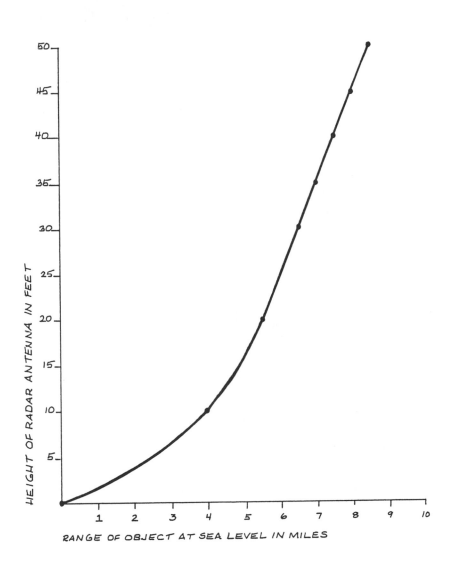

The effect of antenna mounting height on radar range.

twenty feet up the mast may seriously affect the vessel's
stability. Although on a large vessel it may be offset slightly
to starboard to avoid a blind spot dead ahead caused by a
mast ahead of it, to set such a heavy piece of equipment
high aloft and off center too is unrealistic in a small boat. In
a sloop rigged with a short boom, the scanner can be

mounted on legs standing on the afterdeck. Even though this may be aesthetically distressing, it may be not so distressing as giving up the radar.

Although height above the water is an advantage, the accompanying chart shows that the greatest advantage is derived from heights up to about 15 feet. Some further advantage is often gained by refraction of the radar waves, caused by atmospheric conditions, permitting the set to see objects which are over the visual horizon. Finally, of course, the height of the target is as important as the height of the receiver.

The display should be kept away from the compass but, at least in a powerboat, should be near enough the helmsman's position so he can use it if necessary. The cockpit of a sailing vessel clearly has no place for a radar display unit, but wherever it is placed, it should face forward; that is, objects on the vessel's starboard side should appear on the right side of the screen.

Wiring must be well insulated, supported to prevent chafe, and of adequate size. If the run is long and the wire necessarily too big for the terminal, it can be taken to a junction box and a smaller wire run the short distance to the terminal. Obviously, all connections should be bright and tight.

When the set is properly installed and functioning, the navigator must become familiar with it. What appear to be lines, clouds, and vague shapes on the screen must be equated with the visible landscape. The viewer must realize that he is seeing in the scope only what bounces back to the scanner, not necessarily what is out there. For instance, a small sailboat with a good radar reflector may return a much stronger echo than a 60-foot wooden fishing vessel coming straight on. A steel bridge at a distance will return a hard, sharp line that might be mistaken for a breakwater. Two breakwaters overlapping will not show the channel between them. A hill with buildings on it and a long, shelving beach in front of it may reflect the buildings and not the beach, suggesting that the vessel is much farther offshore than is the case. A round, wooden buoy may return a scarcely discernible echo, whereas a steel buoy with a radar reflector may twinkle as it goes up and down on passing waves. The motion of the observer's boat may confuse the reception as well. Lobster trap buoys, driftwood, cresting waves, and vessels' wakes may give a snowy look to the screen, called "sea clutter," in which a small wooden boat, for instance, may be invisible. In short, the observer must take advantage of clear, daylight weather to look at the scope and at the scene to become acquainted with the different kinds of echoes returned.

Then, too, he must realize that when he is underway, he is dealing with relative bearings; that is, the screen shows the bearings of objects relative to the vessel's heading. If he is headed on a course of 40° and sees an object bearing 320° on his radar screen, he must add his course to the relative bearing to get the true bearing to plot on the chart—in this case, 360°, or north.

As the vessel proceeds along the shore, the shore appears in the scope to be going astern by the vessel. To locate your position, you must not merely glance at the scope but also plot the direction and distance of the target on the chart. To tell whether you will clear the ledge off the point, you must plot a succession of positions unless you are perfectly sure that your compass course is actually your course over the bottom. Accidents happen most often to those who are perfectly sure. To be certain of your location at any time, plot a cross bearing either by taking the bearings of three objects or by taking their distances.

When your vessel is moving and you are observing a moving target, the situation becomes far more complicated and less susceptible to evaluation by a quick glance at the display. For instance, if you are moving at six knots, following a vessel dead ahead of you, also moving at six knots, that vessel will appear to be stationary. If he alters course 15 degrees to port, he will at first appear to remain stationary and then very slowly but with increasing speed move off to port at 90 degrees to your course. He has

A diagram of a hypothetical situation in which two vessels with radar are on converging courses. At 1, **A** sees **B** on his screen at a range of 5¾ miles. Both vessels are making 12 knots. After 2½ minutes, at 2, their bearings are unchanged, and after 5 minutes, at 3, the bearings are still the same. **A**, seeing the bearing unchanged and the range reduced to 3⅞ miles, slows to 6 knots. At 4, 2½ minutes later, the bearing has changed only 2 degrees. After another 2½ minutes, at 5, it has changed only another 3 degrees, not enough to appear significant on **B**'s screen. At that point **A** alters course 45 degrees to starboard for 2½ minutes. At 6, the bearing has changed 12 degrees and **B** knows that **A** has accorded him the right of way. In another 5 minutes he will cross **A**'s original course, and **A** may resume his original course and speed.

46

not changed his course by 90 degrees as he appears to have done.

If the target vessel is approaching you at six knots, it will appear to be approaching at 12 knots, the sum of your speeds. If he alters course 15 degrees, the change will at first be imperceptible; then the vessel will appear to be headed at 90 degrees to your course but with a rapidly decreasing range. Actually, it may be some time before you notice any change in his course, for your own vessel may not be holding a perfectly steady course. Anyone who can steer within about 5 degrees in a rough sea is indeed gifted.

A crossing situation presents the same sorts of problems. If a vessel appears to starboard and if his bearing remains unchanged, and if he appears to be moving directly toward the center of your screen, you must assume that there is danger of collision. You might slow down, according the other vessel his legal right of way. However, on neither radar screen will a change be apparent at first, for the bearing will change less than aberrations in steering. The privileged vessel, thinking perhaps that he has not been seen, may then alter course and speed to pass astern of you, an excess of caution that may lead to collision. If instead of merely slowing down, however, you alter your course by 45 degrees, he will see the change at once and hold his course as the law requires. In all cases where there is doubt, actual positions of targets should be plotted on charts; all changes in course and speed should be made long before actual risk of collision exists and should be radical enough to be clearly understood. Note that the current Rules of the Road require the privileged vessel to maintain course and speed until *in extremis*, and specifically forbid turns to port.

The *Stockholm–Andrea Doria* collision dramatically illustrates these points. Although the facts have never been established to everyone's satisfaction, an analysis of the disaster may be instructive. The two vessels were approaching each other on nearly reciprocal courses at night,

Andrea Doria bound west in the fog and *Stockholm* bound east in fair visibility. Both ships were using radar, but on neither was any one officer assigned to continuous observation of the scope. *Andrea Doria* was making about 20 knots and *Stockholm* about 18, so they were approaching each other at a combined speed of 38 knots. At a distance of 12 miles, each was visible on the other's screen. At this time they were 19 minutes apart. *Andrea Doria* had noted that the target, although not plotted, was 4 degrees to starboard when the vessels were 17 miles apart and was steadily increasing its angle to starboard as the ships approached each other. When they were only 3½ miles apart, with only 5½ minutes to meeting time, *Andrea Doria*, still in the fog, expecting a starboard-to-starboard passing, changed course 4 degrees to port, an imperceptible change on *Stockholm's* radar.

Aboard *Stockholm*, *Andrea Doria* was seen to be 12 miles away, slightly to port. *Stockholm* plotted *Andrea Doria's* position and assumed a port-to-port passing with a mile to a mile and a half between ships. This means that the blip on *Stockholm's* screen was only 4 degrees to port. *Stockholm* changed course 2 degrees more to starboard, making a more generous allowance for a port-to-port passing. Actually the two vessels were approaching each other directly, each seeing the other on her radar screen to the north of her true position and each altering course imperceptibly to the south for safety's sake.

When *Andrea Doria* broke out of the fog, the vessels were only about a mile apart. It was stated at the hearing that *Andrea Doria's* radar had shown *Stockholm* consistently to starboard, that *Stockholm's* running lights were seen to starboard, and that a starboard-to-starboard passing seemed appropriate. A hard turn to port was ordered.

Aboard *Stockholm*, *Andrea Doria's* position had been plotted consistently to port, and when her running lights appeared, a conventional port-to-port passing seemed appropriate. *Andrea Doria* was already committed to a turn to port but had not yet turned enough to make this

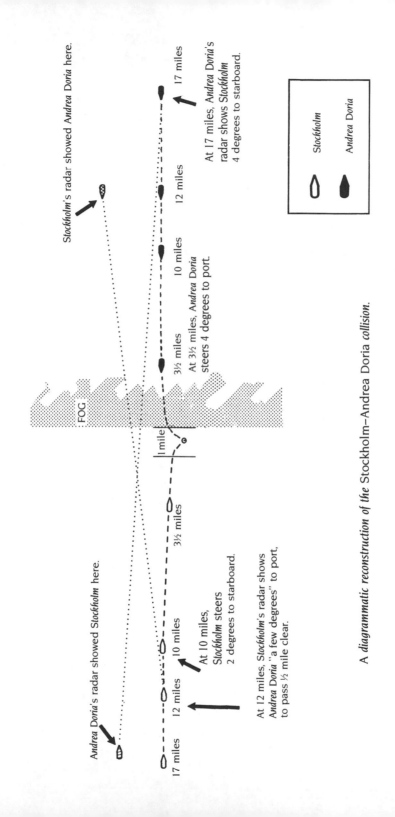

A diagrammatic reconstruction of the Stockholm–Andrea Doria collision.

Stockholm's radar showed *Andrea Doria* here.

17 miles

At 17 miles, *Andrea Doria's* radar shows *Stockholm* 4 degrees to starboard.

12 miles

10 miles

At 3½ miles, *Andrea Doria* steers 4 degrees to port.

3½ miles

FOG

1 mile

3½ miles

At 10 miles, *Stockholm* steers 2 degrees to starboard.

10 miles

12 miles

At 12 miles, *Stockholm's* radar shows *Andrea Doria* "a few degrees" to port, to pass ½ mile clear.

17 miles

Andrea Doria's radar showed *Stockholm* here.

Stockholm

Andrea Doria

apparent. *Stockholm*'s hard turn to starboard then made collision inevitable.

Thus, it is evident that in all cases where there is any doubt, actual positions should be plotted on the chart and changes in course and speed should be made early enough and decisively enough to be readily apparent.

Despite the need for caution and judgment, the experienced radar operator does, indeed, have a window through which he can see in fog and darkness. The skipper of an excursion boat brought her down the narrow, tide-scoured, rocky Sasanoa River at night in the fog with one hand on the wheel, one hand on the throttle, and his face in the radar scope all the way. The mate, standing lookout forward, saw nothing whatever during the whole trip.

Many yachtsmen now use the Whistler or "belly radar." This instrument hangs around the operator's neck and expresses the returning echoes not as light on a screen but as sounds in a set of earphones. A sensitive listener who has used the instrument often can tell the nature of the target and its distance and bearing by the pitch and volume of the signal.

Even the experienced, however, are sometimes led astray. On one yacht, running for a buoy in the fog, a member of the crew experienced with the belly radar stood on the foredeck listening carefully to a return that he judged to be the buoy. Just as he expected it to materialize out of the grayness, another vessel appeared on an opposite course, headed right for him, on its foredeck another experienced operator with a radar set around *his* neck. Each thought he was running for the buoy, but the buoy was somewhere else.

We can say about electronic aids to navigation, then, that although they may be valuable, they are subject to various weaknesses and misinterpretations and so are at best supplementary to clock and compass, not substitutes for them. To be useful, they must be practiced with in clear weather and their possible aberrations and limitations must be studied. The skipper who would rather sail his boat than gaze at an electronic display on a pleasant afternoon might prefer to stay with clock and compass, and with log, lead, and lookout.

6

Plotting
the
Course

Our first concern in plotting a course to be sailed in the fog is to pick a mark that will be easy to find: one that will not put us in a dangerous position should we deviate slightly from our course or miss the target, and one from which we can head for another safe and easy mark. Short courses are to be preferred, even if they take us somewhat out of our way, and bells, whistles, and gongs are most desirable marks. As one fisherman observed years ago, "Them spar buoys are awful dam' silent." A bold shore, that is, a steep rocky shore with deep water close to it, is also a good mark, for the surf will break loudly on it, and if you ease in slowly, you will see the loom of it before you are in danger. Let us assume, then, that we are running from buoy A to bell buoy B.

Plotting the Course

What course do we give the helmsman when we leave buoy A and dive into the fog, hoping to find buoy B? The problem is not extremely complex, but it requires careful attention to avoid falling into foolish mistakes, mistakes easily made while one is bending over a chart table in the cabin of a small boat in a seaway.

First, lay down the base course on the chart with parallel rule or protractor. If your compass suffers from a little deviation on this course, you may ignore it at this point in the calculation.

Next, measure the distance, using the latitude scale on the side of the chart. One minute of latitude equals one nautical mile. Most charts have the minutes of latitude divided into tenths, and these serve very well for fractions of miles. Do not use the longitude scale at the top or bottom of the chart.

Let us suppose the distance is 3.5 miles and the course is due north. Now, estimate your speed. If this is to be a passage under power, let us assume a speed of 5 knots.

From speed and distance, calculate the time it will take to go from A to B. The basic formula expressing the relationship between rate (speed), time, and distance is $RT = D$. That is, *rate* in knots multiplied by *time* in hours equals *distance* in nautical miles. This formula you should memorize. It is as much a part of a navigator's mental equipment as the multiplication table. If it is not already deeply etched on your cerebral cortex, write it on a card and tape it to the chart table.

If $RT = D$, then $T = D/R$; that is, time in hours equals the distance in nautical miles divided by the speed in knots. So our time on this run will be 3.5 miles/5 knots = 0.7 hours. Now, 0.7 times 60 minutes equals 42 minutes. We will, then, be 42 minutes making this passage if our speed remains constant.

Now we find in the Current Table that there is a tidal current setting us to the northwest at ½ knot. If we will be under the influence of this current for 0.7 hours, we will be set 0.7 hours times 0.5 knots, or 0.35 miles. Therefore we must head 0.35 miles to the *southeast* of B so the tide will set

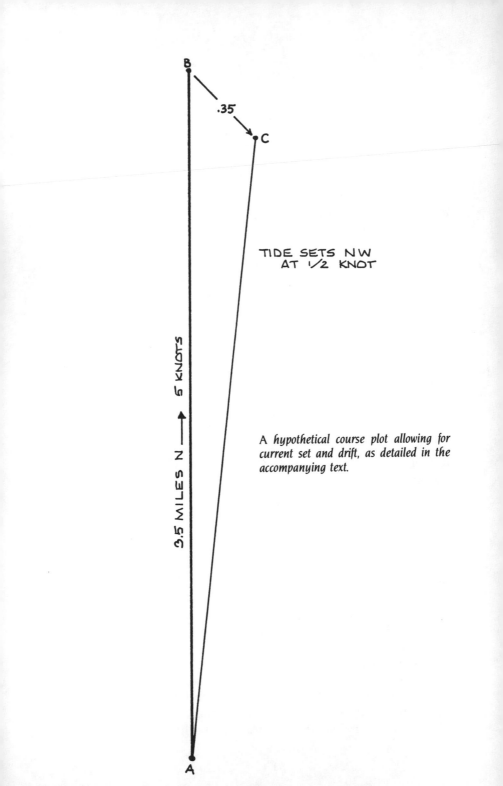

B

.35

C

TIDE SETS NW
AT 1/2 KNOT

5 KNOTS

3.5 MILES N

A hypothetical course plot allowing for
current set and drift, as detailed in the
accompanying text.

A

us down on the buoy. We draw a line 0.35 miles long on a southeast course from the buoy B and label its end point C. Draw AC on the chart and plot the course. It comes out to 007°, or about N ½ E.

At this time we apply the correction for deviation. If your compass adjustor has found an easterly deviation, it means that the north point of your compass has been moved to the east of where it should be and will read a lower number of degrees than would a compass without deviation. Therefore you must *subtract* the deviation from the charted course to get the course you should steer. One is tempted simply to remember, "East is Least; West is Best," and always subtract easterly deviation. However, one must also remember that this neat rule only applies when converting a charted course to a compass course. When going the other way, plotting a compass bearing on the chart, for instance, the rule is reversed. It is wise always to think which way the compass card is moved and how this movement applies to the problem of the moment.

When we leave buoy A, then, if we have no deviation, we tell the helmsman to steer 007°. We will be *heading* along line AC but will actually be *moving* somewhat crabwise along AB.

To determine our time of arrival at B, we now measure AC. The tide running to the northwest will be helping us on our way to some extent, illustrated by AC's being shorter than AB. AC measures 3.18 miles, as nearly as one can measure it. Since a hundredth of a mile is only 60 feet, the measurement is too fine to be consistent with our approximate knowledge of our speed and the speed of the tide, so we round it off to 3.2 miles: 3.2 miles/5 knots = 0.64 hours = 38 minutes to reach buoy B. The mathematician can get really fussy now and say that inasmuch as we are in the tide only 38 minutes, not 42 minutes, the tide will set us a *little* less, so BC will be a *little* shorter, which makes AC a *little* longer and our course a *little* more northerly. This means our time will be a *whisker* more than 38 minutes . . . and so on, deep into a calculus problem.

For practical purposes, however, 38 minutes and 007° will do very well. When the clock reads 33 or 34 minutes, one would shut off the engine and listen anyway, and the fraction of a minute and the fraction of a degree would become irrelevant.

The important points to remember about this simple method of allowing for tide are three:

1. Be sure to lay off BC in the *opposite* direction to that in which the tide is running.
2. Remember that you will actually be traveling along AB, north, 000°, although you will be heading 007° magnetic. Therefore, expect to encounter any buoys or ledges charted on AB, not on AC.
3. Don't worry about hundredths of miles. Remember that this entire operation is the process of reaching a correct conclusion with insufficient evidence.

Of course there are many other ways of solving this simple geometrical problem. It can all be done by trigonometry and programmed into a calculator, for instance. One advantage of the graphical solution, however, is that you can see exactly what you are doing at every step and you can tell whether it makes sense.

Estimating Positions

As you sail the course, you should keep track of your progress on the chart, laying out your courses and distances and making allowance for tide, leeway, and steering error. This process is called dead reckoning by the most eminent authority, Nathaniel Bowditch. A sardonic humorist declares that it is called dead reckoning because it is usually dead wrong. The purist limits the term "dead reckoning" to positions determined by course and distance only, omitting consideration of other influences. All he knows about that position is that he is sure he is not there. After making allowances for tide and leeway, he establishes an "estimated position." These refinements of language seem to help us little. Most navigators arrive at an estimated position by dead reckoning, including all the influences they can think of, and hope that it is pretty nearly correct.

Some of the other factors besides tidal current that can enter into the calculation are leeway and steering error. If you are sailing, especially with the wind forward of the beam, perhaps an allowance should be made for leeway, the vessel's slipping sideways to leeward under the pressure of the wind and seas. Experience will tell you how much to allow, but to make a quick guess, after the helmsman has settled on his course, stand forward of the compass and look astern. Observe the angle between the wake and the lubber line. Adjust your course to windward by the amount of the angle. In general, beginning navigators are inclined to allow too much for leeway. Be conservative.

Under sail, especially with a strong breeze on the quarter, most helmsmen will steer an average course a little to windward of what the navigator asks for. As the vessel charges ahead on a sea and dives into the one ahead, she tends to swing toward the wind. The helmsman counters this tendency, usually a little too late. As the vessel returns to the course, he eases the helm so she comes back about right but is shoved to windward again by the next sea. Seldom does he fall to leeward of the course as often as he is driven to windward of it. Correction for this error is a matter of guesswork. In some cases one simply needs to expect the mark a little to leeward. In extreme cases, perhaps half a point, 5 degrees or more, should be included in the calculation. On a long offshore run the factor is likely to be much more significant than on a short run in protected waters.

Finding the Mark

Finding a bell buoy or a whistle to windward in the fog, under sail, introduces all the sources of error already mentioned, as well as the possibility of overstanding the mark and passing to windward of the buoy, a position from which you cannot hear it. Certainly the cautious navigator would not sail about in the fog looking for a can or a nun except on a very short course. The secrets of success appear to be short tacks, no longer than two or three times the limit of visibility. Keep a careful plot of each tack by clock and compass. Check your reckoning with the depth sounder and listen carefully all the time, especially in the quiet moment after you have filled away on a new tack. As you approach the buoy—or where you think the buoy ought to be—shorten the tacks and redouble the listening. You will be to leeward of the buoy and stand a good chance of hearing it.

Of course if there are islands, ledges, or other marks on either side, they will help you to keep run of your position as you hitch along. A bold shore with a lighthouse, a wharf, or a prominent house is an excellent resource. You can simply tack out until the shore is almost invisible and then tack back. Beware, however, of going out of sight of the shore, for when you tack back, you may have bypassed the mark you were looking for.

In laying out a course, then, the navigator will choose marks that are close together, easy to find, and unlikely to turn an error into a disaster. He will make his calculations on the basis of the most complete information he can assemble. He will be as careful as possible not to make stupid mistakes. He will realize when he has finished his calculations that navigation is an inexact science and will keep a careful record of his progress on the chart and in the logbook.

Finally—and I wish this could be printed in red—despite the best instruments, the greatest care, and the most thorough mental discipline, there are times when discretion is the better part of valor, when the foggy day is best spent over the anchor:

When it is really choking thick, with a wind off the water packing the stuff in ever thicker;

When it is cloudy above the fog so there is little likelihood of its burning off;

When you are in strange waters where you will not recognize what you see dimly;

When your course must run among shoals and ledges unmarked by bells or whistles;

When the tide runs hard and unpredictably;

When there is a heavy sea running that could hammer your boat to pieces in the event of a grounding;

When your crew is inexperienced or fearful;

Don't go. Stay where you are.

We were lost one afternoon at high water with a going tide in a fog so thick that the Vinalhaven steamer, after navigating successfully from Rockland by radar, could not find her slip in Vinalhaven harbor. We underestimated the tide, mistook one headland we had never seen for another equally unfamiliar, got into a nest of half-tide rocks, bounced off one, stuck on another, but fortunately sailed her clear. We anchored, guessed, speculated, blundered about from island to island for three hours, went ashore and asked a party of clam diggers where we were, and at length made a safe harbor in the falling dark. It was a long afternoon! Better we had not tried it.

7

Sailing the Course

The best—indeed the only—way to acquire skill and confidence in the fog is through experience. As the old man said, "Knowledge earned is better than knowledge learned if it don't come too dear." In this chapter we will make a run in the fog from Cutler to Trafton's Island, Maine. This is a real experience. Notes quoted from the logbook were indeed written in the logbook at the time. Details and comments are added with the wisdom of hindsight. If you follow the chart as you read the text, you may perhaps profit from the vicarious experience.

A Fog Run

My wife, Mary, my son, Bob, and his new wife of only two weeks, Cindy, were cruising in our Friendship sloop *Eastward*. We had been into Passamaquoddy Bay and up the New Brunswick shore to Dipper Harbor, and had felt our way into Cutler the afternoon before in a dungeon of fog. We had used up most of our vacation time and were obligated to get back to the westward soon.

I woke early and from my bunk could see through the hatch a gray and featureless sky. Fog dew dripped from the rigging, tapping on the deck in a melancholy, arrhythmical pattern. Big drops hung from the boom. I could hear the horn on Little River Light, muted by the island between us, and the soft complaint of gulls standing on weir stakes waiting for something good to happen. A few lobster boats had gone out earlier, but there were no sounds of activity ashore. I really could see no valid reason for stirring up my crew right away.

However, I knew we really ought to move along to the westward that day, and I went over the possibilities in my mind. The tide runs hard in those eastern Maine waters and sometimes in unpredictable directions. The shores are steep and rugged and there are a great many ledges and half-tide rocks. A look at the chart will show that a run through Cross Island Narrows, across Machias Bay to Foster Channel, through Roque Island Harbor, and out to the Cowyard would be a nightmare in the fog. Swift tides and narrow passages among islands and ledges that all look nearly alike and the complete lack of noisy buoys make this a difficult country for the man who "ain't acquainted that way." The wiser move would be to go outside where Cutler whistle, Libby Island, Mistake Island, Seahorse Rock bell, and the bells and whistle buoys in Western, Pleasant, and Narraguagus Bays would guide us.

In due course I turned the crew out and fed them a large and leisurely breakfast, hoping for a bit of a scale-up as the day advanced—what the coasters used to call "a good chance along." Nothing cheerful happened, though, so at about 9 o'clock in a thick fog and flat calm we felt our way down Cutler Harbor under power and found the nun at the entrance.

9:27   NUN IN CUTLER HARBOR   C.   ESE (112°) TO BELL.   LOW WATER AT MISTAKE ISLAND   12:30

The tide, then, was at full ebb at nine o'clock. However, it

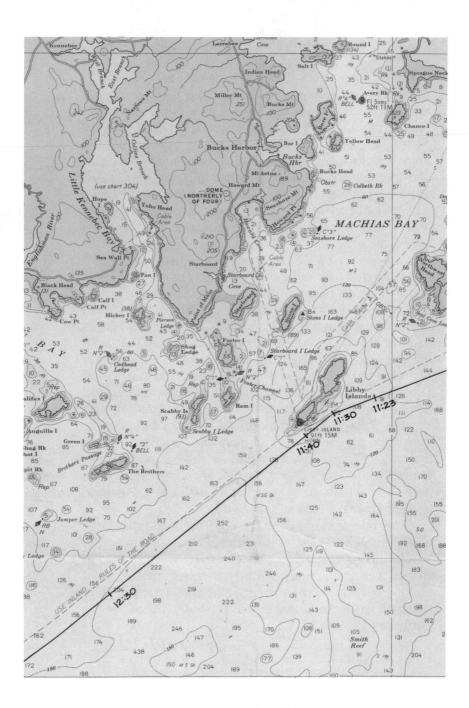

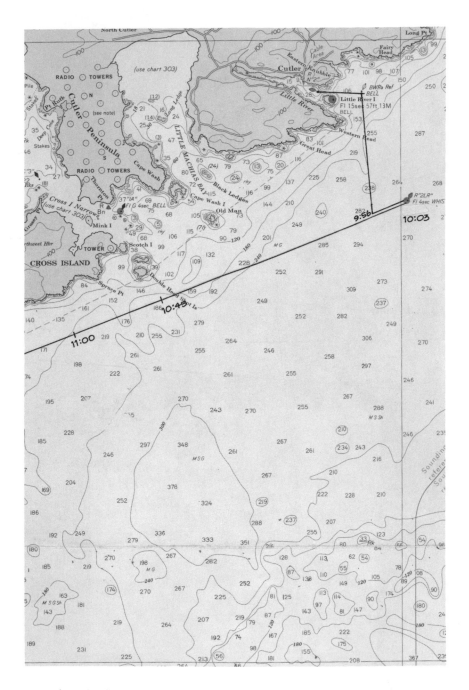

Chart of a day's run from Cutler to Trafton's Island, Maine, showing the coastline and course plots referred to in this chapter.

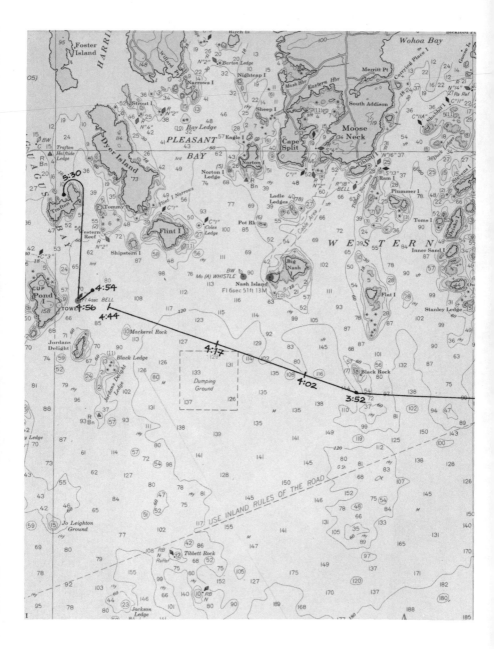

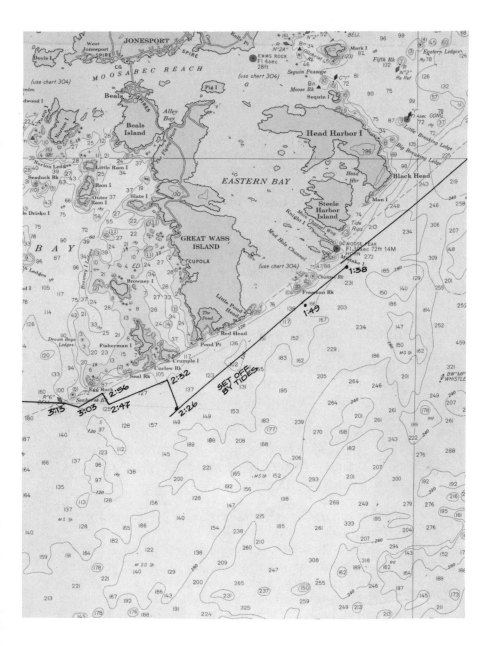

was only a short run of three-quarters of a mile to the bell, and the tide would be running out of Cutler Harbor along our course. I made no allowance for it.

9:35   BELL   C.   S ½ W (185°) FOR WHISTLE

We had taken eight minutes to go three-quarters of a mile from the nun to the bell. Our normal cruising speed is five knots. This time is about right when you count in a fair tide.

The course from the bell to the whistle on the chart is S ¼ E (177°). By steering S ½ W (185°) I was allowing three-quarters of a point, about eight degrees, for the tide. That works out to one-quarter mile in 1.9 miles, or allowance for a tide of about one knot running to the southwest.

9:56   C.   EAST (90°)   REALIZED I HAD ALLOWED FOR TIDE THE WRONG WAY

I had run 21 minutes with the tide setting me one-third mile to the southwest and had allowed another one-quarter mile. I was then over half a mile east of the whistle.

10:03   CUTLER WHISTLE   C.   W (270°) FOR LIBBY ISLAND DISTANT ABOUT 9¼ MI.   TIDE RUNNING W AT ABOUT ½ KNOT

It had taken us seven minutes to push up against the tide to the whistle.

This is an illustration of how easy it is to make a stupid mistake. I had owned the boat for 10 years, had made numerous fog runs, had taken her that summer from Boothbay west to Cuttyhunk and Nantucket, back outside the Cape and across to Maine, and then east to the Bay of Fundy. The three days previous to this one had been thick. Certainly I was familiar with the boat, the chart, and the run of the tide in the Bay of Fundy, yet that silly error had crept in. I have noticed that when such errors are made, they are usually made at the beginning of the day. Fortunately this one was not lethal and my crew excused me, although it may have shaken them.

The course from Cutler whistle to Libby Island is almost due west. The tide would be running with us, not across our course, perhaps setting us offshore a little as it ran out of Machias Bay. Libby Island was equipped with a powerful diaphone, so we should be able to hear it easily as we approached. There are no off-lying dangers. The distance is 9¼ miles. At 5 knots we should be off the light in 1 hour and 50 minutes, without allowing for the ebb tide. I estimated it at about 1 knot, although it seemed to be less at the whistle.

We settled down for two hours or so of running in the fog. Mary steered, giving full attention to keeping the sloop on course, staring steadily at the compass, looking up from time to time to rest her eyes, averaging very close to a course of west but swinging two or three degrees each way as the long swells shouldered *Eastward* one way or the other.

Bob stood forward, leaning against the mast or sitting on the forward end of the house, clammy foghorn in chilly hand, fog dew dripping off his hat brim, occasionally blowing a lonesome bleat, listening for a horn, an engine, surf, the Libby diaphone, whatever could be heard, and looking into the grayness, watching one sea after another roll out of the fog ahead, into our little circle, lift us, ease us down, and vanish into the fog astern—each sea the same, yet each a little different. No sound but the steady chunking of the engine and the wash under the bow. Suddenly a puffin burst out of the water alongside and panicked off into the fog, looking like a little headwaiter with a big red nose, running for the last bus—a bonus for the lookout.

Cindy, just relieved from lookout duty, was below, struggling into a sweater in anticipation of a half hour at the wheel. Her oil coat swung from a hook, the lamp rocked in its gimbals, the clock ticked on, quite unconcerned with fog.

The navigator, still stinging from having applied the tidal correction the wrong way, was considering whether to try for the Cowyard, Mistake Harbor behind Knight's Island, or to push on for Cape Split or Trafton's Island—the considerations being the time of day, the tide turning to the eastward against us, the dangers close to the shores, the distance to be covered the next day, the state of the water tank and the food locker, and the feelings of the crew. This was supposed to be a vacation, a posthoneymoon good time.

10:45 POT BUOY. 185 FEET. TIDE RUNNING WEST AND A LITTLE NORTH   STOPPED TO LISTEN   HEARD NOTHING

We would have come a little over four miles by this time. This would put us on the shoal making off of Cross Island, a not unlikely place to find a lobster trap. However, we were too far off Cross Island to hear the surf and still too far from Libby to hear the horn.

11:00   HEARD LIBBY DEAD AHEAD   TIDE SWIRLS APPARENTLY WHERE TIDE RUNS OUT OF MACHIAS BAY BY CROSS ISLAND

11:23   HORN CLEARLY AUDIBLE   120 FEET

11:30   100 FEET

11:33   94 FEET   C.   W by S ½ S (253°) FOR MISTAKE ISLAND   9½ MILES   HORN SOUNDS HIGH

Again I made no allowance for tide, since it would be with us for the first part of the run, then slack, and then beginning to run against us. We settled down again for another two-hour run.

12:30 STOPPED TO LISTEN MOOSE PEAK (Mistake Island) A WHISKER TO STARBOARD NO BOTTOM

We were probably in the deep water outside the mouth of Englishman Bay. Here the navigator steered for a bit while Mary fired up the stove and produced a fine hot lunch of soup and a sandwich. A cup of soup warms the hands, strengthens the stomach, and cheers the heart.

1:38 MOOSE PEAK ABEAM OVER A HALF MILE OFF DEPTH OVER 200 FEET

The half mile is a guess on the basis of the sounding. It might have been as little as a quarter mile, since the 180-foot contour runs about a quarter mile outside the light.

Here the navigator decided to press on. We had already passed the Cowyard, and the shores of that harbor are studded with ledges. Knight's Island did not seem very attractive, although the deep water and bold shores of Main Channel Way would have led us in. The tide was turning against us, but it was the time of the moon when the tides were not at their swiftest. A course inside Western, Pleasant, and Narraguagus bays would be a little out of the full run of the east-west tide and where a coming tide might possibly be of some help to set us up the bay. There were two bell buoys and a whistle more or less on the course. If the following day should be thick as well, we could make a short run of it or even lay over a day. Crew morale seemed good and there appeared no need to get to a store. Anyway, the only store was in Jonesport and that was out of the question.

The problem now was to find the bell on Seahorse Rock. I did not want to get in close enough to the cliffs to follow the shore. It could have been done. I had done it once before, right in the backwash of the breakers, and had found several outcrops from the cliffs frightfully close. With the thick fog pressing in on the shore, the roar of the surf, the confused sea in the tide and the backwash, and the uncertainty about those ugly black, weed-hung rocks with the seas breaking over them, I preferred to stand off.

I planned to follow the 120-foot contour, which runs well clear of the cliffs, does not lead one into Eastern Bay, and passes close outside Seahorse Rock and inside the bell. The log entries show how we steered west until the soundings dropped off into deep water, and then north again until they shoaled up.

1:44   190 FEET   MOOSE PEAK WELL ASTERN

1:49   C.   W ½ S (265°)

2:26   NORTH   100 FEET

2:32   120 FEET   STOPPED TO LISTEN

2:35   W ¼ S (267°)

2:47   170 FEET   NORTH

2:56   W ¼ S (267°)

3:03   HEARD BELL TO WEST   STARTED UP AFTER A BRIEF LISTENING STOP

3:13   C.   WNW FROM BELL   NO VISIBLE TIDE   WNW FOR SHOAL SOUTH OF BLACK ROCK   2½ MILES   NO ALLOWANCE FOR TIDE   ETA 3:43

It is 5½ miles from Moose Peak to Seahorse Rock, and it had taken us about 1½ hours, evidence that the tide was beginning to run against us, although we had spent some time running north to keep close to the 20-fathom line.

We now headed off across Western Bay toward Black Rock, about three miles away. Black Rock is a rather small, high, black, rocky island outside other dangers and all by itself. It is quite bold, with only one half-tide rock to the south of it, which at low water would be bare if not breaking. The 10-fathom curve lay close enough to it so that we could hear the surf, and far enough from it for safety. A considerable area of 10 to 20 fathoms lay to the south of the rock, so we would know by the soundings when we were up to it. The tide might be partly against us and it might be setting us to the north, up the bay. In either case we should be able to find the 10-fathom shoal, only three miles away. The notation about the tide was obviously important to me at the time.

3:52   SOUNDINGS DROPPED BELOW 120 TO A CLEAR 130   C. NW ½ W (310°)

We had found the shoal, crossed it, and were clearly on the western edge of it. We had not seen Black Rock, but we did not have to. We had a fairly good idea of our location and were clear of any possible obstruction. We now headed for the bell off Pond Island, five miles away. The bell was an excellent mark because it lay close to a big island with a bold shore. If we missed the bell, we would make the island and could feel our way along it until we found the bell.

The navigator decided in favor of Trafton's Island and against Cape Split because the entrance to Cape Split is beset by ledges and there is no noisy buoy off it. Also, Cape Split is a somewhat rolly anchorage. The crew was tired, had suffered from the motion, and wanted, above all other terrestrial satisfactions, a quiet night.

4:02   STOPPED TO LISTEN   FAINT SURF TO EAST

4:05   STARTED UP   85 FEET

The surf was on Black Rock. The sounding indicated we were on the tail of the long shoal making off Nash Island.

4:17 STOPPED TO LISTEN NASH ISLAND NE ½ N
(40°) SOUNDINGS NOT CLEAR

4:20 STARTED UP

We stopped in the hope of hearing Nash Island whistle in
order to see how far along we had come on our course to
Pond Island bell. The whistle was most reassuring.

4:44 STOPPED TO LISTEN SURF TO THE SOUTH
NASH ISLAND TO THE EASTWARD NO BELL 85 FEET

4:48 STARTED ON

We were now well by Nash Island. The surf to the south was
on the steep cliffs of Jordan's Delight. It was evident from
the sounding and from the clock that we were closing in on
Pond Island, but we still could hear no bell. It was getting
on toward the end of the afternoon. While we had a good
two hours of daylight left, I was beginning to view with
some concern the distinctly unpleasant prospect of being
caught out in the fog at night. The crew was tired from a
long day on the water under some anxiety, for we had felt
our way from horn to bell to the sound of surf with no sight
of land.

4:54 STOPPED TO LISTEN HEARD BELL NEARBY

4:56 C. WSW (247°) FOR BELL

4:58 C. NE by N ¾ N (25°) FOR EAST SIDE OF
TRAFTON'S ISLAND
NO TIDE 1.6 MI. = 12 + 7 = 19 MINUTES

We went on then for another half mile and listened again.
With triumph and delight we heard the bell close by,
bearing west southwest, suggesting that the tide had set us
up the bay a little. We felt our way up to that lovely bell,

which we could have valued no more had it been made of purest gold, and we squared away for the bold east shore of Trafton's Island. We observed no tide running by the bell but suspected there might be a current running up Narraguagus Bay between Trafton's Island and Dyer Island. We made no allowance for it because it would be behind us, hustling us along.

On schedule we heard the surf, saw the dark loom of trees, followed the shore to the north end of the island and slipped into the quiet cove. We dropped the anchor, reversed the engine to dig it in, and shut the engine off.

With inexpressible relief we welcomed the quiet. The darkening water lay around us without a ripple. The tall spruces stood silently over the steep rocks. A shag flew busily across the cove and a seal surfaced silently to inspect the new arrival.

5:30   ANCHORED AT TRAFTON'S ISLAND

Piloting Versus Navigating

The foregoing account represents the scientific navigator's approach to a rather long outside run in the fog. The inside course was abandoned before the start because the country was not very familiar. All the islands around Foster Channel look pretty much the same—bare and grassy islands shaped like domes—and one half-tide rock looks like another at first glance. In familiar waters, however, a different approach is possible. Here, the pilot recognizes this red cottage with a tower on the corner, that island with a crooked, weather-beaten tree on the south end, the smell of the ledge where shags and gulls nest. The pilot knows that there is usually a scale-up among the islands of the Thread of Life. He recognizes the characteristic deep tone of a certain bell buoy and he recognizes the lobster buoys of his neighbor who sets around a certain shoal. He knows about where he is at all times and can step from one known mark to another with confidence, knowing what he will make and recognizing where he is if he misses his mark by a little.

The cruising yachtsman, as he passes among the islands in fair weather, would do well to notice such peculiarities and to make notes of them in his log. All islands do *not* look alike, even off the sandy shores of Cape Cod. It is *not* true that when you have seen one half-tide rock, you have seen them all. The following brief account of a passage under sail up Penobscot Bay with a local fisherman will give some idea of the pilot's approach as opposed to the navigator's:

> As we sailed up the bay before a southeast breeze, a thick blanket of fog shut everything from sight. I was sent to the bow with a foghorn and with orders to report everything I saw or heard, and I couldn't see more than 30 yards ahead. Soon I heard ospreys screaming but paid no attention to them, when the captain hollered, "Hear them birds?" "Yes," I answered. "Well, them's fish hawks and we are just off the Porcupines, for that's where their nest is." He headed a little to the eastward and soon I shouted, "I hear surf ahead." He said, "All right, come aft—that's the rote on Hard Head; there ain't any place in the bay where the waves hit a flat cliff with the boom they make on Hard Head." Very shortly after that we picked up the loom of Eagle Island and heard the bell on the lighthouse there.

A man with whom I used to go lobstering when I was a boy seemed to find his way about as if by a sixth sense. We would leave the harbor in the foggy dawn and, without compass or watch, run off into the fog. Presently one of his lobster buoys would appear out of nowhere. For several hours we would go from buoy to buoy hauling traps and gill nets. Then he would head for home, and shortly we would break out of the fog at the harbor mouth. I asked him one day whether he had a compass. He brought out of the cuddy a battered box compass with a big bubble in it and set it on the engine box as we headed for home. With every bang of the make-and-break one-cylinder engine, the compass jumped a bit, and with each jump the card turned. As I watched, it went all the way around from lubber line to lubber line.

I observed that the instrument wasn't of much help. He agreed and added, "There's most always a roll making up the bay from the south in the summertime. Keep that on your port quarter and you'll make all right."

I should add that our traps were set in a line along the edge of a shoal about a mile offshore. If he hit the line anywhere, he would find one of his buoys and from there work along the line to the others. From the end of the line he would make the harbor every time with the swell on his port quarter.

One foggy morning my wife and I were anchored at Point Lookout on Isle au Haut, listening to the fishermen talking on the shortwave radio. One voice came through in great distress, from the skipper of a sardine carrier who was supposed to pick up a load of herring from a weir in Duck Harbor, a tiny slit of a cove surrounded by a maze of ledges. The burden of his cry was "Breakers!" and "I ain't acquainted around here." He was clearly frightened. Presently a calm voice came in.

"Hey, Cap, what does that ledge look like?"

"I dunno. Just rocks."

"Does it have a big square boulder on the south end?"

"Yes, it does."

"That's the Brandies. Now go slow and easy out by the north end and keep clear of the lobster traps."

"Thanks, Cap." A momentary silence.

"You'll find another ledge to starboard right away. That's still the Brandies. It's in two pieces. Go out by the northern end of that." Another silence.

"I'm by it, Cap. Now what do I do?"

"Now steer east three-quarters south. You'll find more traps." Brief silence.

"I got the traps. Now what?"

"Look and listen to starboard. You hear a ledge?

"OK, Cap. Now steer east by south three-quarters south." A considerable pause.

"Hey, Cap, I got a big ledge ahead. You know I ain't acquainted around here."

"That's all right, Cap. That's Haddock Ledge. Follow around to the nor'ad of it and you'll see a big white rock to port. That's Duck Harbor and you're home free. Just come alongside the weir and pump out."

"Thanks a lot, Cap. You know I ain't acquainted around here."

8

Lost

When as a boy I asked the old man about sailing in the fog, he answered, "It's all right if you make all right." But what if you don't?

Before you run out your time, you will stop and listen. Let us suppose you hear nothing. You run on, and when your time is out, you stop again and listen. Still no buoy. Then perhaps you run on for another half mile in the hope that you are running a little behind your time and will find the buoy. Again you stop and listen. Still nothing. Shut off the engine or heave to, so that there is not even a bow wash to distract you, and listen for a full five minutes. Sounds in the fog can be tricky. You can wait in silence for what seems an age and suddenly hear quite clearly a single stroke of a bell or the shriek of a whistle as a bigger wave than usual raises the note an octave.

While you drift and the crew keeps listening, reread your log. Replot your course. Did you make some foolish mistake in arithmetic? Did you make a correction for tide, deviation, or leeway in the wrong direction? Is it a moon tide? Could you have made insufficient allowance for it?

Making a Box

If all these and any other explanations you can think of come up negative, you will have to "make a box." Turn at 90 degrees to your former course and run for half a mile, let us say five minutes. Write down your course and time and any hints you can get from depth finder, pot buoys, sounds of any kind, even smells. Again stop and listen with engine shut off.

Turn 90 degrees to the reciprocal of your base course so you are running parallel to it half a mile to one side of it. Again listen. Turn 90 degrees again. This should bring you in five minutes to where you were when you ran out your time. If the tide is running hard, you will have to make an allowance for how much you were set while making the box and listening.

If you are *still* lost, make another box on the other side of your course from that on which you made the first box. If you are dreadfully unlucky, you may have to make four boxes before you find the buoy. Don't ask about what will happen if you don't find it after four boxes. You *will* find it. I suppose you could extend the sides of the boxes to cover a larger area. If you get into shoal water, you can anchor and wait for something good to happen, or you can go to sea. To adopt Columbus's policy and head west until you sight a large continent can lead you into worse trouble than being lost in deep water. However, on a short coastal course you are most unlikely to miss your mark by over half a mile.

When you are listening, listen with the greatest concentration for whatever you can hear. The faintest hint may be a great help. Gulls screaming on a ledge, birds singing in the woods, a lobsterman hauling traps, his motor idling and then speeding up and idling again, may lead you to something you can identify. Lobster traps are ordinarily set in the summer in less than 100 feet and sometimes in very shoal water around ledges and islands. The sudden sound of a distant horn, previously inaudible, may lead you to conclude that you have come out from behind a point or island which was previously masking the sound. A distant motor that grows and fades again may be a ferry on a known route or a fisherman heading for home. Automobile horns or people shouting and laughing may suggest a nearby tourist attraction. Even a barking dog may give you a hint that will lead you to a right guess.

Log of a Confused Afternoon

The following gives the account of our missing and then finding the Schoodic whistle one summer afternoon. The accompanying chart shows where we must have been, the courses having been laid out afterward, working back from the whistle. Apparently we missed the mark on the run from Petit Manan because the strong ebb tide set us far to the south. We expected to arrive at the whistle at 3 o'clock.

2:45   STOPPED TO LISTEN   SURF DIMLY AUDIBLE TO STARBOARD   ONE CLANG OF A BELL   WHISTLE APPARENTLY FAR TO PORT   FOG VERY THICK   NO WIND AT ALL   VERY CONFUSING

The bell must have been the one on Brown Cow, the surf on Schoodic Island. I mistakenly assumed that if we could hear these, we must be to the north of our course, even though there was a moon tide running hard to the southwest for which I had made no allowance.

2:55   STOPPED TO LISTEN FOR 5 MINUTES   WHISTLE VERY FAINT MORE OR LESS AHEAD   WHALE PUFFING TO PORT   NO BOTTOM

The whistle was not ahead at all but on our starboard quarter. This was possibly wishful thinking or else the whistle was so faint that we could not tell where it was.

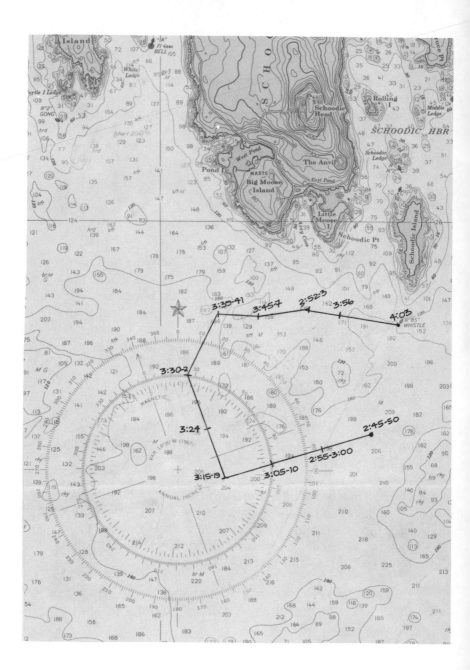

A portion of the U.S. Coast and Geodetic Survey Chart #306, showing a reconstructed plot of a confused run in the fog off Schoodic Point, Maine.

3:00 STARTED UP

3:05 LISTENED ANOTHER FIVE MINUTES SOMEONE HAULING TRAPS AHEAD VERY FAINT WHISTLE

Again the bearings of the sounds were deceptive. It is most unlikely that anyone was hauling traps ahead unless they were on the ridge in the middle of Frenchman's Bay.

3:10 STARTED UP

3:15 LISTENED 4 MINUTES LOBSTER BOAT WAY TO STARBOARD OTHERWISE NOTHING NO BOTTOM C. NORTH

By this time I must have concluded that we were far to the south of the buoy because we had no bottom at 200 feet and we heard a lobster boat to the north.

3:24 STOPPED AGAIN EGG ROCK NNW C. NORTH

This was a brief stop because we heard the horn on Egg Rock quite clearly. It proved to be an accurate bearing and placed us well to the south of the buoy. I guessed that we had just come out by the shelter of Schoodic Point and that was why we had not heard it before, so I guessed also that we were east of our actual position. We continued north.

3:30 STOPPED AGAIN HEARD WHISTLE FAINT TO NE C. NE

3:32 STARTED UP NO BOTTOM

At last we heard the whistle clearly enough to get a more or less accurate bearing on it—with considerable relief!

3:39 STOPPED HEARD WHISTLE TO ESE

3:41   STARTED UP   C. ESE   STILL NO BOTTOM

3:44   BOTTOM AT 120

3:45   STOPPED

3:47   QUITE CLEAR   E BY S   STARTED UP   BOTTOM AT 140

3:52   STOPPED   CLEARLY AUDIBLE   SE BY E ½ E

3:53   STARTED UP ON THAT COURSE

3:56   STOPPED   HEARD IT JUST TO STARBOARD

3:56½   STARTED UP   SE BY E ½ E

4:03   MADE WHISTLE

The reader, if impressed by the apparent obtuseness of the navigator, must bear in mind that he did not have the lines on the chart making very clear to the reader exactly what was happening.

Expecting the Unexpected

Strange and unexpected things can happen in the fog, things which in that mysterious ambience seem to challenge our belief in a solid and reliable world. My son, looking for a bell buoy less than a mile off the powerful horn at Whitehead, ran down the bearing from the light, met two other boats also looking for the buoy, and was about to conclude that the buoy had recently sunk when one of his crew heard a faint "clunk." He ran down the sound and found the buoy with three of its clappers missing and the fourth broken short off so it no longer touched the bell but hit the stop behind it.

My uncle, with a carefree crew, was off Thacher's Island near Cape Ann one warm, muggy summer afternoon when the fog shut down. They didn't know where they were but they knew they wanted to get to Gloucester. They pushed on in a generally westerly direction for a while until they heard an engine. Out of the fog came a local fisherman headed for home.

"Which way to Gloucester?"

"Thataway. Fifteen-a minoot-a."

"What is the course?"

"Thataway. Fifteen-a minoot-a."

And off he chugged into the fog. My uncle tried to follow, but the fisherman was much faster and soon was out of sight and hearing. Then the fog seemed brighter to starboard and took on a greenish hue. A very impolite voice shouted, "Hey, you! This is private property. Get to hell out of here." My uncle willingly complied.

As night fell they heard the horn on Eastern Point on the end of the breakwater at Gloucester, rounded the breakwater and anchored in the black dark.

During the night there seemed to be a good deal of bell ringing in the vicinity, to which the tired mariners paid small attention. On waking in the morning and looking out the hatch from his bunk, my uncle was astonished to see what appeared to be steel plates and rivets on the gray sky. Presently an anchor swung into view. He sprang to the hatch and found he had anchored close under the bow of a battleship on maneuvers.

On another occasion I was towing another yacht across Frenchman's Bay in the fog. We made the bell off Old Whale Ledge all right, and then the bell off Otter Cliff. We then planned to follow the bold shore around to Seal Harbor. First we had to cross Otter Cove. The cove is less than a half mile wide, with bold shores. It seemed reasonable that any westerly course would make the other shore, so we started across. Halfway across, out of sight of both shores, I saw a ledge under us. It looked like white granite and I seemed to see the weed waving over it. One of the crew dropped the sounding lead over the side. No bottom at five fathoms! I tried to turn away from the ledge but the skipper of the yacht on the end of the towline had seen the ledge too and was trying to dodge it on his own. This pulled our stern around uncontrollably. We got clear of the ledge without striking and then saw another. We seemed beset by ledges where the chart showed 78 feet of water.

I was rattled. I began to question everything. Was it really Old Whale Ledge bell we had found? Was this really Otter Cove? There was no other similar cove on the southeast side of Mount Desert. Could some geologic catastrophe have occurred to make a ledge appear where for centuries there had been no ledge? Meanwhile, we were dodging between the ledges, being yanked by the towline at unpredictable moments.

Then the fog scaled up and we saw both shores and the South Bunker Ledge outside, and beyond question we knew where we were. We saw no more ledges and proceeded very carefully to our anchorage.

The next day, hitchhiking across to Bar Harbor on an errand, I was picked up by a National Park truck. When I had told my story, the driver laughed so hard he had to stop the truck. They were building a causeway across Otter Creek. Clay had washed down the creek and made streaks in the water.

All phenomena have logical explanations. Be sure you see what you are looking at. Don't panic.

9

Collision

The sea is so big and boats, even the largest, are so small that one would think the chances of actual collision to be small, too. Such, however, is not the case. There have been so many tragic accidents that seamen have developed over the years a generally accepted code of rules for protecting themselves and each other. As vessels developed from sail to steam, increased in size, and changed in maneuverability, the rules were slow to change. In 1972, however, the International Marine Organization held a convention of representatives of maritime nations and adopted the International Regulations for Preventing Collisions at Sea, known in government language as 72 COLREGS. These were amended in 1983 and became effective as United States law on December 23, 1983. They apply to all United States vessels on the high seas and to all vessels in United States coastal waters outside lines of demarcation drawn across the mouths of large commercial harbors. Inside these lines, Inland Rules prevail, but in most cases these conform to COLREGS. Both sets of rules are published in

Navigational Rules—International and Inland, available at most chart outlets and from the Superintendent of Documents, U.S. Government Printing Office, Washington, D.C. 20402. The code number of the book is COMDTINST M16672.2A. While there is no longer a requirement that you carry a copy of the book aboard, it is well to have one over the chart table for quick reference. The rules for navigation of small boats in "conditions of restricted visibility" are so simple, they are worth extracting and memorizing:

RULE 5.   In any condition of visibility every vessel shall maintain a proper lookout.

RULE 19.   In conditions of limited visibility proceed at a safe speed and avoid turns to port if another vessel is ahead. Avoid turns toward that vessel if she is abeam or abaft the beam.

RULE 35.   A vessel under power shall blow a prolonged blast every two minutes.
A vessel under sail, towing or being towed, adrift, constrained by her draft or her ability to maneuver, or anchored and fishing shall blow a long blast followed by two short blasts.
A vessel at anchor shall ring a bell.

Proceeding in the Fog

Beyond compliance with these rules, the skipper will naturally take every precaution to prevent collision. To this end, as well as to make navigation easier, it is much safer to proceed under sail in the fog than it is to use the engine. Assuming that there is enough wind to maintain reasonable speed and that one can fetch the next mark, a vessel under sail is fully as maneuverable as a vessel under power and, most importantly, can hear better. Although the government requires the blowing of horns and ringing of bells as a safety measure, a great deal more safety is achieved by listening than by blowing. A lookout should be stationed forward, away from conversation and engine noise—if any—and aft of the sound of the bow wash. He should concentrate most of his attention on what he hears.

Unless it is blowing hard, and seldom does it blow hard when fog is thick, one can hear a long way on the water. The rumble of an engine, a horn, or even people talking may carry over water reasonably well.

One thick afternoon my wife and I were beating down Muscle Ridge Channel between the shore and a tangle of islands and ledges. We stood in until we heard the white-throated sparrows singing in the trees and stood off until we heard the gulls screaming on the ledges. On one offshore tack we suddenly heard someone sneeze and someone else exclaim "Gesundheit!" We never saw the other vessel running up the channel with a fair wind and were in no danger of collision, but we knew they were there and we had a part in their day.

Your lookout, then, should listen more than he should blow. However, to comply with the law, he should blow. The common reed fish horn is all right for sailing about in narrow waters among small boats, granted that the lookout has stout breathing apparatus; but for outside work where big fishermen and steamers may be encountered, something with more decibels than a fish horn is needed. The high-pitched horn mounted on a can of Freon is much better than a fish horn. Hold it away from people's ears and point it toward suspected danger. The most powerful horn you can have is the best.

Besides listening, the lookout might as well look, although for the most part there isn't much to see. In the fog one moves in a small, moving circle of visibility. Waves roll into it and roll out of it. A gull or a shag may fly through it. A long-sought buoy will swim into it. The edges of the circle are important. A buoy or an island may just touch that edge, visible dimly for a moment and then gone. Its presence may be just the hint the navigator needs. A vessel, if it is to be a danger, will probably show up ahead or astern; if ahead, it will be visible for only an instant before a collision.

Coming west toward the bell off Petit Manan we were motorsailing in the thick fog, hard on the wind, crashing through the chop, the sun making a dazzle of the fog all around. We knew we were near the bell, but we hadn't heard it. Indeed, we were about to shut off the engine and listen for it, when out of the fog dead ahead burst a sloop under spinnaker, running down east before the wind. She had just passed the bell and was sailing the reciprocal of our course. We were approaching each other at a combined speed of perhaps 12 knots, which gives one about 4½ seconds to react if visibility is no more than 30 yards. We twisted out from under her bow to windward. Her owner had not seen us at all from behind his spinnaker and stared aghast as a sloop from another century flashed by 10 yards from his cockpit and was gone again into the fog astern. Had my wife not been alert on the foredeck, we could have had a major shipwreck.

Communication between the lookout and the helmsman is particularly important. It should be understood that the lookout will not point to perceived danger but shout and motion decisively with his whole arm in the direction in which the helmsman is to steer. Also he should *turn around* and shout "port" or "starboard." It is no use to stand with your back to the helmsman and shout. One acquaintance of mine was thus instructed and sent forward, told to point to port and shout "Port!" if he saw bottom to starboard and vice versa. When his moment came and he saw bottom suddenly, he did not point; he shouted neither "port" nor "starboard." He jumped a foot off the deck and screamed "Jesus."

As a reward for a half hour of intense concentration, listening, staring into the fog, and blowing the horn, the lookout should be given a respite before being assigned to further duty.

Safety Devices

Another defense against being run down is the radar reflector. One type consists of three squares of aluminum arranged to interlock so that each crosses the other two at a right angle. From whatever angle a beam of light or a radar impulse strikes the reflector, the reflector will send it right back whence it came. Another type is a sphere composed of concentric layers of metal foil so arranged that the radar pulses are reflected. The spherical reflector is more expensive but less likely to get fouled up aloft, and is said to be more efficient. Whichever type you use, it should be hoisted as high aloft as possible. This is not so much to make it visible on a radar screen at a great range as it is to prevent its being lost in sea clutter on the screen.

Another device recently developed by International Marine Instruments Inc. of 40 Signal Road, Stamford, Connecticut 06902 is the Combi-Watchman. This consists of two parts. The first is the Omni-Antenna, a little five-inch by seven-inch box mounted anywhere on the boat, which gives an audible and visual alarm if any vessel within five miles is operating a radar. The second part is a radar direction finder, 7½ by 3½ by 3½ inches, which tells the direction from which the radar pulses are coming. If more than one radar is operating in the vicinity, the direction finder will distinguish among them. If this instrument is as good as it is claimed to be, it would be very useful in negotiating busy shipping lanes, despite its cost of about $350.

If you have a radar installed on your vessel, you must tame it before the fog shuts down. Chapter 5 of this book includes many of the precautions to be considered, the main point being that radar tells you only the distance and relative bearing of the target at the moment the beam crosses it. To get the course and speed of the target, you must watch it for several minutes and plot its positions on the chart. If risk of collision is suspected, make large and definite changes of course and speed long before it seems necessary, for relative bearings change very little at first and may not be noticed for some time.

The Whistler radar, carried hung around the operator's neck and expressing direction and distance of a target by variations in pitch and intensity of sounds, is said to be a great help in the hands of an experienced operator. Considerable practice is necessary, however, before it can be depended upon.

The VHF radio is another useful means of avoiding trouble. Large vessels moving through crowded waters often broadcast their position, course, speed, and intentions. If you miss the announcement and hear the deep, terrifying roar of a steamer's whistle or the heavy thrum of a big engine, call on Channel 16 for the vessel in such-and-such a position. Large vessels are required to maintain a radio watch and usually do. I have found them most cooperative in stating their intentions and in telling whether we appeared on their radar scopes. Other small boat skippers have been less fortunate.

Special Hazards

A dangerous place is likely to be the outer buoy at a busy harbor. Vessels of all sizes may be making for it from different directions. Running for the bell off the entrance to North Haven in Penobscot Bay one foggy day, we encountered simultaneously and close to the buoy the North Haven car ferry, a big motorsailer, a small sloop just out for a sail, and a lobsterman hauling traps. Off Schoodic whistle at the entrance to Frenchman's Bay and Bar Harbor we found a big power yacht orbiting the buoy at high speed, uncertain of the next course to steer.

Approaching a large commercial harbor like Boston or Saint John, New Brunswick it is well to call Harbor Control on Channel 16 to report your approach and intentions and to ask for an assessment of the current traffic situation. If there is a traffic separation scheme, indicated by tinted areas on the chart, keep well away from those areas. They are not for small, low-powered boats but for big vessels. In entering such a harbor from the outer buoy, a small boat can run up the line of channel buoys, leaving red buoys to port or green buoys to starboard, keeping just outside the main steamer channel. There is usually plenty of water for a small boat on the "wrong" side of the buoys. If you do this on entering the Cape Cod Canal from Buzzards Bay, stay *close* to the buoys, for in some cases there is very little room between the sand flats and deep water.

One old-timer, beating up a narrow channel between flats in the thick fog, hailed the skipper from forward to report the presence of a flock of ducks ahead.

"Be they swimmin' or be they walkin'?"

"They be walkin'."

"Hard a-lee."

Commercial traffic on the West Coast of the United States is said to be more of a problem than it is on the East Coast, except perhaps for the entrances to Boston and New York harbors. Puget Sound and San Francisco Bay are churned day and night by big steamers. Such a vessel in a traffic separation pattern or a narrow channel can do little to avoid a small boat, even if the small boat shows on its radar. Most of the steamers, however, keep to their regular channels and the cautious yachtsman will avoid these.

Another problem unique to the West Coast, particularly to Puget Sound and the waters north of it, is the deadhead. A deadhead is a log, one end of which has become waterlogged so that the log floats vertically. It has very little buoyancy, sometimes floating with the end just awash. As it gets even more waterlogged, it will sink slowly. When the butt hits bottom, the log may then rise very slowly until the end breaks the surface. The end loses what little buoyancy it has as it comes out of water, and it then begins slowly to sink again. These logs may be fifty feet long or longer and they are immensely heavy. Hitting one is about the same as hitting a rock. They are not on the chart, of course, as they drift about with the tide, and in many cases it is impossible to see them even on a clear day. The best one can do is to keep the sharpest lookout possible and recognize the peril.

Night Sailing

Nighttime adds another whole dimension to fog, for when darkness falls, the circle of visibility disappears and one can see nothing at all. You might as well have your head in a bag. Even bright lights are smothered at a range of a few yards. I have been lost inside a tight harbor just rowing out to my boat on a foggy night. I eventually found her, but not by seeing her anchor light. It was invisible until I bumped alongside.

No one who goes to sea for pleasure would sail a boat among the ledges and islands of a broken coast at night in the fog. Anchor. Stay where you are.

Offshore or on an unencumbered coast it is possible to move at night in the fog. Courses should be set for noisy buoys—bells, gongs, or whistles—or for buoys off light stations with fog signals. The danger of collision with other vessels, debris, or fish traps is much greater after dark; and if you miss your mark, run out your time, and find no buoy or sound of a buoy, there is almost no alternative but to stand offshore until daylight. Certainly, wandering about listening for the low moan of a whistler in the black dark offers little chance of success. If the buoy is well clear of obstructions, a carefully organized search pattern is possible, but the careful navigator will anchor or go to sea.

In daylight, however, most situations can be dealt with as they arise, and time is always on your side. We were beating out of Boothbay Harbor on Windjammer Day, one of the great occasions of the summer, when the cruise schooner fleet visits the harbor. With the fog so thick, it was doubtful that many would come in, but we had sailed around inside the harbor where the fog had scaled up, looking at those who had anchored there the night before. Then we hardened sheets to beat out again and plunged into the fog. Visibility was very limited, but we could hear motors all around us. One we recognized as a ferry whose route we knew. He was no problem. Another was abeam, coming closer, but dropping slowly astern. A long blast of our horn and two short ones slowed him down and we soon saw his bow poking cautiously out of the fog. When he saw he was clear of us, he resumed his moderate speed. Another motor could be heard astern, a heavy one, moving slowly. We blew. Then the shore loomed up ahead. We tacked and blew again and the heavy motor astern swung after us. Was he chasing us? We gave him the horn again. He nearly blew us out of our shirts with a giant blast, his motor speeded up, and an excursion boat slid up alongside, his radar whirling. A public address system gave his passengers some picturesque information about us and he faded away, to return from time to time because there wasn't much else to show his passengers that day. While this was going on, we heard a long blast and two short ones ahead, and then we heard them again, coming closer on about the same bearing. A grayness on our weather bow took shape as the schooner *Roseway*. Under her lower sails she came sliding up the harbor on the starboard tack. As we were on the port tack, we tacked at once, hailed her skipper, and she slipped back into the fog, her passengers staring. We tacked back, heard a lobsterman pulling traps, his motor idling and then speeding up. Then a voice:

"There's another one of them now!"

"No, that's just the *Eastward*."

And into our circle of vision slipped an anchored powerboat waiting to see the schooners come by. She should have been ringing a bell, but no one seemed concerned about it.

It was a busy morning, but there was no great peril, and

by listening thoughtfully we could take necessary action. One youth in a Boston Whaler did come at us much too fast. We blew, but we knew he couldn't hear us. As he burst into our circle, he saw us, wheeled sharply away and was lost again. But those are the chances you have to take. Some people don't know the rules, wouldn't care if they did, and don't know enough to be scared.

10

An
Account
of a
Passage
Down
East

This is the account of a passage from Gloucester, Massachusetts to Bremen, Maine, in the course of which we made almost all the mistakes of omission and commission possible for people who had been on the water as long as we had.

The skipper, an old friend and ally of mine, had bought from one of my colleagues a Sparkman & Stephens sloop about 37 feet long, fast and close-winded under sail but with only enough power to get her home in calm weather. He had bought her in Gloucester in September, and we planned to take her to his home in Bremen over the Columbus Day weekend.

The radio prediction was for calm, clear weather with a moderate southwest breeze. I had visions of a carefree, fair-wind passage before a warm southwester. We went aboard Friday night and turned in under a brilliant starry sky. The morning, however, dawned calm, cloudy, and murky. We went alongside the gasoline float, filled the tank and several plastic jerry cans with gasoline, motored through the Annisquam Canal, and laid a course for the Isles of Shoals. A light northeasterly breeze struck in. Under mainsail and genoa we could just lay our course, so we hung up the radar reflector on the backstay and washed along over a calm sea at about 4½ knots, dodging duck hunters in dories anchored amidst their decoys.

We had already made several mistakes. First, one should never, under any circumstances whatever, put gasoline in a plastic container. Some plastics are soluble in gasoline and quickly disintegrate. Also, gasoline sloshing in a plastic container can generate static electricity, which may create a lethal spark. Second, we had hung our radar reflector on the backstay instead of hoisting it high aloft. At a height of perhaps only ten feet, it would be lost in the sea clutter on a large vessel's radar. Finally, we had not calculated our times and distances to see where we might be at the time of mid-October's early sunset.

After an hour or so beneath a cloudy sky, visibility closed down to about a mile and the wind dropped off somewhat. We started the engine and chugged on through the murk and showers, occasionally getting some good out of the sails as the wind came and went from north northeast to east northeast.

We passed through the Isles of Shoals early in the afternoon, continued to York Ledge, and headed for Cape Porpoise's lighted whistle buoy, about 18 miles away. By this time it was about three in the afternoon, the breeze had strengthened again, and somewhere off Kennebunk the gas tank ran dry.

The fill pipe came through the deck inside the cockpit coaming. We put a funnel in the deck plate, I held it steady, and the skipper began pouring from the jerry can. There was no spout, just the screw top on the can. With the chop that had built up, we slopped some of the gasoline on the deck, whence it ran down into the cockpit.

"Don't worry," we said. "It will run out through the cockpit scuppers."

Fortunately the damp day was not favorable for the build-up of static electricity or we would have blown up at this point. We had bought ourselves plenty of trouble short of that, however. The gasoline we had spilled did indeed run down the cockpit scuppers. But the scuppers discharged underwater, so that gasoline floated on the water standing in the scupper pipe. Every time the sloop sat her stern down in a trough, the water came up in the pipe and regurgitated gasoline onto the cockpit floor, whence it ran back again to float in the scupper pipe. Furthermore, in the middle of the cockpit floor was a large, threaded deck plate, perhaps ten inches in diameter, to provide access to the stuffing box and steering gear. We became concerned lest gasoline leak through this deck plate and create an explosive situation below. Accordingly, we did not want to start up the engine again until we were sure that the mixture of gasoline and water washing across the cockpit floor had not gotten below. Remember that this was a new boat to both of us.

In the course of the pouring operation, during which I had been holding the funnel, some of the gasoline had slopped up on my hands and on the cuffs of my jacket sleeves, and more had soaked into my sneakers and socks from the cockpit floor. So when I went below to sniff around for gasoline, I carried the smell with me. Our wives, who had been below, declared that the whole boat smelled of gasoline, as of course it did as soon as I came down the hatch. Consequently, we did not dare touch the starter button.

About this time, too, we received a radio weather report predicting heavy northeast winds for the night. This added to our anxiety, but there did not seem to be much we could do about it. We thought about going into Cape Porpoise for shelter.

We continued sailing in a gentle northeast breeze, beating slowly up toward where we thought we should find the Cape Porpoise whistle, now with a tack in toward Kennebunk, then with a tack offshore, making slow progress, seeing nothing and hearing nothing, and keeping run of our position as best we could.

The dull afternoon shut down into dark shortly after five

o'clock, and the fog shut down with it, making the night as black as tar. The skipper's wife challenged the fates and lit the stove to put on a fine corned beef dinner, which was one of the best things that anyone did that night. The skipper was wound up pretty tightly from anxiety over where we were and what would happen when the northeast gale struck, and I, as navigator, was doing the best I could with insufficient information, for with no depth sounder and in complete ignorance of how the tide was setting us, I was just guessing at our position and I knew it. Neither of us thought of setting watches.

About nine o'clock we heard a faint moan to windward and slowly worked our way up to it, finally seeing the dim loom of the buoy right alongside, with the glow of the light flashing halfway up the mainsail.

We now were sure of our position, but the idea of running for Cape Porpoise harbor was in no way attractive. It was a fair wind for the harbor, and we probably would be able to make Old Prince bell outside the entrance, but beyond that the course lay between unlighted beacons. We would not be able to see Goat Island Light until we were too close to it for safety, and the whole horrible coast would be a lee shore whence there was no escape without the engine. Although we had lighted the stove without blowing up, we still did not dare to start the engine, which was perhaps a measure of our own nervous tension rather than a measure of the actual danger. But under any circumstances, running before the wind for an unlighted entrance encumbered with lobster traps, in the fog, at night, is at best poor judgment.

Our mistakes thus far were impressive: storing gasoline in plastic containers, pouring the explosive stuff at sea into a funnel too small, neglecting to mop up the spill, going below with gasoline on the clothes, lighting the stove when there was any doubt, and letting ourselves get nerved up were all wrong. A hot supper—granted one was going to light lamps and a stove below—and the decision not to run in for Cape Porpoise Harbor were wise. Finding the whistle was partly luck and to some extent good judgment.

Inasmuch as we were not going to run in, we headed offshore on a course for the Portland Lightship. We had heard no more about a gale and the wind had worked somewhat to the east and perhaps a bit to the south of east. The skipper was still tense, could not rest, and steered most of the time himself. We did not set watches. I did not want to quit if he didn't, so we both stayed awake most of the time. My wife, wiser than either of us, turned in for a while, and the skipper took a little kink, until some time about midnight we struck a log a glancing blow. Both came awake with a start, my wife concluding that the old fool navigator had at last put her ashore. I got a little shut-eye later on, but the skipper at the wheel was so tired that he suffered hallucinations and at one time found himself steering the reciprocal of our course. The binnacle light was too bright and perhaps added hypnotism to hallucination.

Early in the morning, long before dawn, I got an RDF bearing on the lightship, and about four o'clock we began to hear the horns on Cape Elizabeth and the lightship. Then we heard the deep, thundering blast of a steamer's whistle. We reasoned that she was steering for the lightship. She was right astern and gaining on us at every blast. The night was still pitch dark, the fog choking thick, and every minute that roaring blast was nearer. We imagined we could hear the rush of a bow wave.

We figured we might as well be blown up as run down, so we started the engine, turned on the spreader lights, blew our feeble fish horn as loudly as we could, changed course 90 degrees, and sprinted for safety.

Although in our nervous and sleepless state we did not think very clearly, we realized at once that no steamer could see our lights very far away nor hear our horn above the wash of her own bow wave. We were in the center of a very small circle, dazzled by our own lights, deafened by our own engine and horn, and quite out of touch with the lightship, Cape Elizabeth, and the steamer. We shut off the lights, slowed the engine, and listened. No steamer. Then we heard the grunt of Cape Elizabeth and the horn on the lightship not far ahead. Still no steamer. We concluded, perhaps too hastily but probably correctly, that the steamer would take care not to run into the lightship, so we took a bearing on the lightship and kicked the throttle wide open. Soon we could hear the horn even above the engine and the wash of the bow wave, and shortly after that we saw the light. The fog scaled up and we saw not one but two steamers lying to near the lightship, waiting for daylight to go into Portland.

That was essentially the end of the misadventure. We set a course for the buoy off Seguin, twenty miles away, welcoming simultaneously daylight, a good breakfast, and a friendly whale. We met no more really thick weather and that afternoon picked up our home mooring.

Between Cape Porpoise and the lightship we had made several further mistakes. We had not set watches, so both the skipper and I were tired, and we had not used the strength of our wives except to provide a supper. Both were quite capable of steering and giving us a break. We had not posted a lookout. Even if we had, he could not have seen that log, but nevertheless, we should have had someone forward looking and listening. We had panicked when we heard the steamer and had totally forgotten that we had a radio we could have used to call the steamer and ask if he had us on his radar. Or we could have called the lightship for an assessment of the situation. We were plain lucky that the fog scaled up when it did and that we did not come on one of the steamers in the dark and fog. Even if we had not run into her, she would have scared us into cardiac arrest. Our navigation, at least, was accurate, and the gale failed to materialize, so the night was quiet enough for us to hear the horns and whistles.

We conclude from this collection of errors that forethought and clear thinking are of the essence. Hunger, cold, wet, anxiety, and lack of sleep are all enemies of clear thinking. Any one of them alone may confuse the mind, and their combination can be frightful.

Set watches. Half an hour at the wheel is enough in fog or

dark. Rotate duties, use all your crew, and allow time for rest. Feed the crew at regular times. Provide oil clothes and extra jackets for those who come ill-equipped. Inspire confidence by thinking carefully, saying little, and moving deliberately.

Finally, to end where we began this book, sailing in the fog is an exercise in good judgment, clear thinking, and mental discipline. It is most satisfying when it is over.

Index